THE REVOLUTIONARY POWER

OF THE
LORD'S PRAYER

ALICE BURNETTE GREENE

Foreword by Kate Harvey Jacobs
Afterword by D. H. Kortright Davis

JUDSON PRESS
PUBLISHERS SINCE 1824

Join our mailing list for updates and special offers.
www.judsonpress.com/mailing_list.cfm

Interior design by Beth Oberholtzer.
Cover design by Danny Ellison.

Library of Congress Cataloging-in-Publication data
Cataloging-in-Publication Data available upon request.
Contact cip@judsonpress.com.

Printed in the U.S.A.
First printing, 2017.

Contents

Foreword

Wow! Just WOW! I always knew that Alice Burnette Greene is an impressive and powerful presenter of God's message, but this book is beyond impressive—it is transformative. I first met Alice in the 1990s when she arrived as an elected representative of the DC Ministers Council to that organization's national senate, a clergyperson whose every word and very being stood up audaciously for God's calling to all Christians. Ultimately she became president of the national Ministers Council and served from 2006 to 2009, an outstanding leader and role model for pastoral leaders in our time.

But this book is not simply a resource for pastoral leaders and religious professionals. *The Revolutionary Power of the Lord's Prayer* is the perfect resource, in the words of the author, "for dedicated disciples who wish to become better equipped to make a positive difference in the world in Jesus' name; it is for Christians who seek to become revolutionary world-changers for Christ."

In this age when the decline of brick-and-mortar retail seems mirrored by the decline in churches and denominations with no way for an online version of Christianity to continue the work in this different time, our world desperately needs a clarion call summoning us back to the authority and hope inherent in the original message of Jesus. Too often, people today respond to Jesus but cannot see how most effectively to live out the role of disciple and transform the troubles of our time into a world of justice and peace. Those people will benefit richly from reading, reflecting on, and discussing this book, and then joining together with others of faith to make all things new.

When an unnamed disciple asked that Jesus "teach us to pray," Jesus responded with the Lord's Prayer, which taught not just words to speak but also expressed a faith to be lived. Alice Burnette Greene has done likewise in a book that responds to our needs, not just to know what Jesus taught and why, but how his way invites, encourages, motivates, and equips us to follow in world transformation here and now.

The book's impact lies in its rare combination of profound emotion that stirs the heart along with intensely deep scholarship that provokes the mind. The comprehensible format is ideal for all conceivable readers, with each chapter focused on a phrase from the prayer. The organization of the chapters presents the focal concept in experiences of real people and contemporary organizations, explores it in the context of Jesus' time, makes it personal in individual reflection, and finally outlines it for group discussion intended to generate action.

As someone who has sought resources for church bodies, book groups, and personal inspiration, I have never before been blessed to find such a gift that unites today's disciples with the original disciples to walk together toward the goal God has for all creation.

None of us can accomplish this goal alone, nor are we called to do so. We are eternally joined together with Jesus and his disciples. I believe that is where the Holy Spirit moves in power, through a phenomenon that scientists have called quantum entanglement. Science has shown us the fundamental unit of physical reality is not the isolated particle but the web, the field, the relationship that binds. Everywhere this web of life binds us together with others so that our prayers on their behalf do not just ascend but reach out. They flow not up to a satellite God to beam down an answer but direct-ly through that web to touch our sisters and brothers who are companions on this journey of life, and together we act.

God has a glorious destiny for creation, a future day when all created beings encircle God. And you know the way of a circle: the closer each point in the circumference is to the others alongside, the closer all are to the center. The closer we draw near one another as created beings, the closer we all are to God, our Creator. The journey toward that day begins here and now, with you and me, through our relationships as we travel through life. We are eternally and quantum-ly entangled, and we will change this world. A resource like this book unites us toward that end.

As Alice Burnette Greene says, "In the Americas, if all 86 percent of the people who claim to be Christians fully understand that God's vision for the world doesn't have any of God's people suffering from entrenched poverty, war, or disease, and if they devote themselves to living like they want that vision to become true, then they will work out a way to make the necessary societal changes no matter what social or economic system controls their countries."

Rev. Dr. Kate Harvey Jacobs
Former Executive Director of
ABC-USA Ministers Council

Acknowledgments

As wonderful as words are, they cannot fully express the depth of my gratitude for those who helped me along the way with this book. My family, friends, and colleagues have provided encouragement, support, food for thought, and the space I needed to allow this book to happen. I appreciate all of you. You know who you are. Thank you!

Introduction

The Lord and Praying

In Chapter 11 of the book of Luke, one of Jesus' disciples asks him to teach them to pray. The prayer that Jesus taught in response to this request is likely the most popular Christian prayer of all time. Known as "the Lord's Prayer," it has been taught to Christians throughout the centuries to be memorized and prayed as an expression of faith. To learn and be able to recite the Lord's Prayer whenever the need is felt is important for Christians. Praying this prayer helps to open us to God's presence, to bring us peace when we are troubled, to remind us of the many blessings that God has provided to us through Christ, and to be dedicated, humble, grateful, and more forgiving.

This short prayer has amazing power to draw us closer to God and to help us through any circumstance we may face. Yet, as with so many of Jesus' teachings, when we study it deeply with sincere faith, this prayer offers so much more. I believe that when Christians begin to understand why Jesus chose the precise words of this simple yet potent prayer, the true power of the Lord's Prayer will be released to change the Christian faith. Not only will Christianity be revolutionized, but Christians themselves will become empowered to revolutionize the world.

The Gospel of Luke emphasizes that Jesus prayed often. He prayed while he was being baptized—that's when heaven opened, the Holy Spirit descended on him like a dove, and God the Father declared his love and respect for his Son (3:21-22). The night before he chose the twelve disciples, Jesus prayed all night on a mountainside (6:12-13). He often got away from the hustle and bustle of the crowds to what Luke calls "lonely places" to pray to God (5:16). He prayed in deep agony on the Mount of Olives before heading to the cross (22:39-45).

I think the disciples must have been impressed by Jesus' commitment to prayer, and that's why they asked him to teach them to pray. I surely am impressed with Jesus' commitment to prayer. Maybe the disciples were thinking what I've thought for some time: If Jesus, who is the faithful Son of God, felt it necessary to pray often, then I surely must need to pray so much more! I suspect some of you have had that same thought.

I'm also sure that Jesus' commitment to prayer was not incidental to his mission. I believe he was intentionally providing an example for those who choose to follow him, including not only the disciples who walked the earth with him, but all of us who claim the name "Christian." Jesus not only taught us the words to pray and showed us the high priority we should give to prayer in our lives, he also showed us how to live the prayer that he taught by how he lived his brief life. So in this book we will examine the words that Jesus taught and their importance as we pray them, and we'll also examine Jesus' example of how to live like we really mean what we are praying when we repeat the Lord's Prayer. Then we will discuss how modern-day disciples are to follow his example.

The Purpose of This Book

This book explores the Lord's Prayer and its significance for dedicated disciples who wish to become better equipped to become a positive influence in Jesus' name. I offer an in-depth study of Jesus' response to the seemingly simple request, "Lord, teach us to pray," focusing intensively on the fact that this request was made by the disciples who had already given up everything to follow Jesus, and who had already been following him for some time. They were not new in the faith when they asked Jesus to teach them to pray!

Jesus would have understood completely what the disciples wanted from him. He knew what they would need in order to do the work he had planned for them. He also knew that they would be greatly challenged by the world, and the struggles they would face. Jesus' response was clearly designed to help his disciples focus on praying for what would be most important to enable them to do his will and what would also help them stay committed when challenged. The Lord's Prayer provides these same important insights for all of us who claim the name "Christian."

Jesus' response to the simple request of his disciples is short and straightforward, but as are so many of his teachings, it is packed with amazing depth and power. If we really want to learn how to pray as Jesus taught, we must understand his purpose in choosing the specific words of this prayer. If we are truly dedicated to following his teachings, we must understand how to live like we really want what we are praying for to happen. We must not only repeat the words, we must understand with some depth what we are praying for so that we can know what to expect when God responds and how to respond to God's blessings. When we understand what we are praying for and follow Jesus' example, we'll find the answer to our prayers. That's when we, as his disciples, will become the revolutionary force that Jesus always intended for us to be in this world.

My purpose in creating this study is to help Christians deepen in faith and in commitment to follow Christ in a way that impacts the world. I want to encourage you to live like you really mean what you're praying—to live like you really want and expect what you're praying for to happen. I want to help you strengthen your faith and your belief that you really can make a difference, and to understand the great and wonderful power that is yours to wield in the name of Jesus. This book is for dedicated disciples who wish to become better equipped to make a positive difference in the world in Jesus' name; it is for Christians who seek to become revolutionary world-changers for Christ.

How This Study Works

I'm presenting the prayer from the Gospel of Luke, a shorter version than that found in Matthew's Gospel. Matthew's version is the one most often taught by the church as the Lord's Prayer. I chose Luke's version for this study, first because many scholars think it more closely follows the original form of Jesus' teaching[1], but mainly because in Luke's account Jesus adds three related lessons to this prayer: the parable about the man who knocks on his friend's door at midnight with a request; the often-quoted "Ask and you will receive, seek and you will find"; and a lesson about what a good father will give to his child. These three lessons provide us with significant insight on how to understand and interpret the prayer.

While the Lord's Prayer is the object of our study, the disciples' request, "Lord, teach us to pray," is the primary key to the focus of this study. So we begin by examining the disciples' request in the first chapter, as well as Jesus' responsive introduction, "When you pray, say. . . ." Following that, Chapter 2 will take a look at the three lessons that Jesus taught after the prayer.

Chapters 3–7 will each focus on a line in the prayer: (3) Father, hallowed be your name, (4) Your kingdom come, (5) Give us each day our daily bread, (6) Forgive us our sins, for we also forgive everyone who sins against us, (7) And lead us not into temptation.[2] Chapter 8 provides some concluding observations about Christians maturing in faith to harness their God-given power in today's world.

Each chapter begins with a "Life in Our Time" story that either highlights people who are doing some exceptional work to bring God's will in the world, or shows some problem in our world that needs fixing. Each chapter concludes with information that will help to deepen your thoughts about some issues we face today and, based on what you have just read, how followers of Christ might respond. This deepening information is followed by individual exercises and questions for group discussion that will hopefully help to further expand and deepen your thoughts.

The stories, information, and deepening exercises are included so that we might keep one eye on the world in which we live as we carefully examine the prayer that Jesus taught. As modern disciples, we must always be aware of our world and our role in it. The information and activities that begin and end the chapters are to help us to stay grounded in the realities that we face, offer some uplifting examples of what Christians are doing, and share some serious and sad facts about societal ills that still must be addressed. My premise is that we are to be involved in making these fixes as today's disciples. Hopefully, the stories and information will spark individual reflection and lively group discussions that encourage you and your churches to become Christian revolutionaries!

I suggest you read this book individually—no more than one chapter at a time—and complete the individual deepening exercises, then take some time to pray and meditate on the meaning of the chapter for your own life. These individual readings can then be enhanced by group discussion of the chapter. The group discussions should bein with a review of the chapter and sharing of personal insights, followed by the group discussion activities and closing with prayer.

My hope and joy will be for those of you who study this prayer to receive the revolutionary power that Christ offers when you follow his way and do his will in this world. No matter where that might take you, I pray that you will be steeped in the tenacious love, impermeable peace, and unbounded joy that only God can provide to guard your hearts as you learn to mightily wield God's power to revolutionize the world.

NOTES

1. See R. Alan Culpepper, "The Gospel of Luke," in vol. IX of *The New Interpreter's Bible*, ed. Leander E. Keck, et al. (Nashville: Abingdon Press, 1995), 234: "The wording of the prayer in Matthew is more polished, and the Matthean version contains seven petitions, whereas the Lukan form contains only five. . . . It is generally agreed that whereas the Matthean wording is more original in places, the Lukan structure is probably closer to the original form of the prayer."

2. I use the 2011 edition of the New International Version (NIV) of the Lord's Prayer found in Luke's Gospel throughout this study. All other Bible quotes are from the New Revised Standard Version (NRSV) unless otherwise indicated.

Chapter 1
The Disciples' Request and Jesus' Response

When the disciples asked Jesus to teach them to pray, they may have had in mind something different from what they received. They asked Jesus to teach them to pray "just as John taught his disciples" (Luke 11:1). In his commentary on Luke, R. Alan Culpepper points out, "By the first century there were set prayers. A devout Jew would repeat the prayers in the morning and again in the evening. . . . Apparently, John had also taught his disciples a set prayer."[1] The disciples may have had a particular type or format of praying in mind, like John taught his disciples. I'm sure that they already knew how to pray by the time they asked Jesus to teach them. Maybe the disciples expected Jesus to instruct them on other facets of praying, like when and how often to pray.

The simple prayer that Jesus taught his disciples may not have been what they expected, but it was crafted precisely to meet their needs. It was designed to get them to focus on what would be most important for them as disciples. The wisdom in this prayer carried them through more than they could ever have imagined, especially after Jesus ascended to heaven, leaving them to carry out his work in the world.

Jesus' prayer has not lost power as it has been passed down through generations. It demonstrates how God's wisdom guides believers in ways that are wholesome for everyone. When we seek to follow the wisdom and guidance of Christ as his first disciples did, we may be taken to places we never expected to go and we may learn new things about faith beyond what we could have imagined. We are given new opportunities to participate in the revolution that God has planned for the world. Our first story shows one way this worked out in the life of a young woman in our time.

Life in Our Time

Rev. Angel Sullivan was in her final year at Colgate Rochester Crozer Divinity School in 2003 when she became the Young Adult Women's Ministries intern for American Baptist Women's Ministries (ABWM). Little did she know that this would start her on a journey where she would find herself "Soul Train" line dancing with Muslim girls in the Republic of Georgia!

Rev. Sullivan's work with ABWM eventually put her on the American Baptist GIRLS [Girls in Relationship, Leadership, and Service] National Leadership Team as the adult Mission and Events coordinator. She was asked to join a group of American Baptist women who had been invited by the Evangelical Baptist Church of Georgia to participate in a cultural exchange that would focus on religious freedom. That invitation was the result of a prior visit to the Republic of Georgia by the former General Secretary of American Baptist Churches USA, Rev. Dr. A. Roy Medley, and American Baptist Women's Ministries Executive Director Virginia Holmstrom.

Rev. Sullivan had a desire to learn about persons of other faiths and an interest in building relationships among people, so in 2014 she joined the first of three spiritual pilgrimages to the Republic of Georgia. The Evangelical Church of Georgia had already begun developing a relationship with the Muslim community in Georgia, where they are both minority religions.[2] The pilgrimage experience was both heart-warming and eye-opening for her.

The Baptists and the Muslims welcomed the American Baptist women with warm hospitality. One portion of the trip found Rev. Sullivan staying in the home of a young Muslim family with two children. During a discussion about faith, she asked the parents, "How do you experience God?" Before the parents could answer, their eight-year-old son, George, responded: "When you really connect with God, you feel God's presence and you know that God is with you."

That was a moment when Rev. Sullivan realized that God is with all people, because she knew exactly what young George was talking about. "If more people were able to sit down, eat together, and talk with each other, they would learn that they really do share similar ethics and that they have more common core values than differences," she said.

Rev. Sullivan returned to the Republic of Georgia in 2015 to attend the International Forum on Religion and Peace hosted by the Georgian Muslims Union. The conference brought in people of different faiths from around the world. Executive Director Holmstrom had been invited to speak about religious diversity and freedom in the United States of America. This time Rev. Sullivan stayed in a Muslim community school for girls. She was delightfully surprised to find that so many of the Muslim women were impressed with her as a woman minister. Her confidence in her own ministry and work soared.

One evening at the Muslim school, the high school girls initiated a spontaneous dance party in their dormitory. Rev. Sullivan was surprised to find herself dancing different kinds of dances with the Muslim girls, including the Hokey Pokey and a "Soul Train" dance line. She didn't expect to find these girls, who normally wore long skirts and hijabs, to be wearing jeans, eating popcorn, and dancing, as she put it, "just like any teenage kids in America."

She knows now that not only did she gain a deeper perspective on who Muslims are, but those Muslim girls also gained a deeper understanding of Americans, particularly African American women ministers. "This is what American Baptist Women's Ministries does so well: building relationships, offering opportunities to get to know other people, and not running from controversial or challenging issues. They truly work toward creating the Beloved Community." In 2015, Rev. Sullivan began an elected term as the national president of ABWM, a position she holds alongside her ministerial profession as a chaplain at a hospital in Florida.

"Lord, teach us to pray"

This was the request that led Jesus to give his disciples what we now call the Lord's Prayer. We deepen our insight about this seemingly simple request and Jesus' response to it when we focus on the fact that the request came from Jesus' disciples. These were the people, both men and women, who had given up their livelihoods, their families, their security, and their comfort to follow the wandering preacher. By the time they asked Jesus to teach them to pray, they had been with him for some time, and they had witnessed much.

They had seen Jesus help Simon Peter catch a boatload of fish where there hadn't been any fish a few minutes before. Jesus had healed a leper, a paralytic, the centurion's servant, and a myriad of others who came to him. He had raised the widow's son from out of his coffin, restored Jairus's daughter from her deathbed, and quelled the storming sea with a few words. He had cast out legions of demons, healed the woman with an issue of blood, and performed many other miracles and wonders. I'm sure that, while watching Jesus wield his power, the disciples noticed that he never used this power to benefit himself. Jesus always used his power to help others.

In addition to witnessing many of Jesus' miracles, the disciples were at his side as he taught with so much power and authority that thousands of people crowded around to hear him. They were at his side when he "stood on a level place"[3] and taught them the beatitudes, love for their enemies, withholding judgment of others, bearing good fruit, and how both hearing and acting on God's words build good foundations for life. They listened as he taught them through parables: about the blind leading the blind, seeing a speck in another's eye when they have a log in their own, and sowing seeds in good soil.

The disciples had also listened to Jesus' intense debates with the Pharisees and other religious leaders. They had likely heard about how Jesus enraged the synagogue leaders in his hometown to the point that they drove him out of town. They had joined Jesus as he plucked grain on the Sabbath to eat, and witnessed when Jesus rebuked the Pharisees who told them they were violating the law. They were there when he had boldly healed the man with the withered hand, in direct opposition to the Sabbath teachings of the scribes and Pharisees who were watching him. They had watched Jesus' example as he forgave the sin of the woman who anointed his feet and at the same time chastised the Pharisee homeowner for his inhospitality.

The disciples had seen it all, and they knew that Jesus was someone extraordinarily special, whom they recognized was from God. They had come to trust that he was truly the Messiah. He was the expected one, the one who would bring healing and hope for the Jewish nation. They were excited about being his followers. They were enthusiastic. They had no doubts about who he was or what he could do.[4] When they called him "Lord," they meant it.

I'm sure they were passionate about being Jesus' disciples, not only because of what they saw him do and heard him say, but also because they themselves had been changed through their relationship with him. In Luke 9 Jesus sent the twelve core disciples to drive out demons, cure illnesses, and preach the kingdom of God. The disciples found they were able to "(cure) diseases everywhere" (verse 6).

But we're also told that after their victorious trial run, the disciples were not able to heal the child with convulsions, they didn't understand Jesus' teaching about being betrayed, and they argued over who would be the greatest among them.[5]

Jesus continued to teach them, however, and in chapter 10 of Luke's Gospel, we're told that he offered them another chance by sending out a group of seventy-two or so of his followers "to every town and place where he himself intended to go." They returned rejoicing because in Jesus' name even the demons submitted to them. Jesus rejoiced with them—I like to imagine Jesus laughing and dancing with them—celebrating their victory over Satan and their promise of heavenly reward. Maybe their dance was similar to Rev. Sullivan's "Soul Train" dance line with the Muslim teenagers!

By the time the disciples asked Jesus to teach them to pray, they had already experienced the powers that Jesus shared with them: the power of his teachings, the power of his authority, and his power to heal. The disciples had complete faith in Jesus and had felt his power in their own lives. Yet, they knew they still had more to learn from the master teacher. They wanted to follow the example that Jesus set for them. They wanted to learn to pray like Jesus prayed, out of their sincere belief that he was the Son of God, and out of a deep and heartfelt desire to be the best disciples they could be for him. And I'm also sure that they asked him to teach them to pray because they saw him pray—a lot.

It's clear that at this point in their walk with the master teacher, the disciples weren't asking to pray for their own comfort and security—they had already left all of that behind.[6] They were not seeking to better their lives in any material way—they had been taught by Jesus not to worry about those things.[7] They did not want to learn how to pray because they feared anything, for they had Jesus right there with them. The disciples asked Jesus to teach them how to pray because they wanted to strengthen their ability to wield the power to cast out demons in his name, to heal the sick, and to teach as he taught. They wanted to strengthen their ability to do the things Jesus wanted them to do. They wanted to be more like Jesus. That's why they were following him, that's why they went out at his bidding, and that's why they asked him to teach them to pray.

Yes, they wanted more power. But following Jesus' example, they didn't want to wield this power to benefit themselves in any way. They were not asking to pray in order to receive any kind of special benefit from God that would make their lives easier. They simply wanted to be enabled to better do the things that Jesus taught them to do. They wanted to do Jesus' will in the world. That's why they asked Jesus to teach them to pray; that was their motivation for making the simple request, "Lord, teach us to pray."

This significant insight will help us to more clearly understand what we are asking from God when we pray the prayer that Jesus taught his disciples. Because his disciples includes both those who walked the earth with him as well as all of us who now proclaim our faith in the risen Lord, this prayer is designed to help us in the same way it helped those first followers of Christ.

"When you pray, say . . ."

Colossians 1:19 reminds us: "For in [Jesus] all the fullness of God was pleased to dwell. . . ." I have often marveled at the idea that all that God is could dwell in a human. Jesus, as God in the flesh, could see and understand things on multiple levels at once, far beyond what our human minds are capable of understanding. I'm convinced that's why sometimes his responses to people seem to be so unresponsive—he wasn't just talking to them as a normal human converses. He was connecting to them in a godly way that the rest of us cannot understand.[8]

I'm sure it was difficult for those who walked with Jesus on earth to understand him when he spoke from the perspective of God because he was speaking from knowledge that took into account everything from the beginning of time into the future and beyond. While talking to his disciples, he was also talking to us, right here and right now, and he was also talking to all who will come to believe in future generations. The words he spoke are to be understood by people in all cultures and throughout all time. That's why his words carry such great depth of meaning, and that's why we can continually mine his words for deeper understanding. Jesus' words speak many volumes.

Because Jesus on earth was God in the flesh, we know that he completely understood all that was going on with his disciples. He understood how they each were formed, what they were capable of doing, their fears and their hopes, what he wanted them to do, and what they were going to go through in order to do it. He knew that they wanted to serve him, he knew that they did not really know what that meant, and he knew the difficulties they would face. Jesus knows all these things about each of us as well.

When Jesus responded to the disciples' request to teach them how to pray, he chose a simple, straightforward template, with only a few clear petitions. He followed up on that model prayer with some teachings, which we'll study in the next chapter. But the simplicity of the prayer is significant in itself. Jesus could have spent time teaching the disciples about the correct physical posture for prayer: standing, kneeling, prostrated, or facing in certain directions. He could have instructed them on what events to pray about. He could have talked about getting their hearts ready for prayer, how often to pray each day, and other various rituals, such as lighting candles or using prayer beads. He didn't focus on any of those things, at least not in Luke's account. Jesus, the God-in-the-flesh master teacher, said simply, "When you pray, say. . . ."

The simplicity of this response doesn't detract from the depth of its teaching. Jesus spoke simply and directly to the disciples, responding to what the disciples wanted and what he knew they needed, because he knew well what was in their hearts when they made their request. He didn't need to tell them not to pray for clothes and houses and food, because he had already taught them not to worry about those things and they had already begun to demonstrate their ability to follow him without anxiety about the necessities of life. He knew they were not fearful, because he had sent them out twice to test them.

He knew that they wanted to be more like him and to do his will. He knew that the words he shared with them would be significant for them, because they were his dedicated followers who were already living like they believed in the prayer that he taught them. He knew that this simple prayer was enough for them to do great works, even more powerful than the works he did when he was on earth.[9]

I am convinced that while Jesus was teaching his first disciples this prayer, he was also thinking about, speaking to, and teaching all of us—all who would come to follow him through the ages. He wants us to continually seek to understand the depths of truth to be found in this simple prayer, so that we may grow in our understanding of how to live in ways that share the good news about the kingdom of God, and so that we will be strengthened in our faith and knowledge of the power that we can wield in Jesus' name.

We, too, are asking Jesus to teach us to pray. We, too, are seeking to learn how we can be the best disciples that we can be. We, too, want to be strong enough to overcome our challenges. We, too, want to understand how to wield power in Jesus' name—revolutionary power, transforming power, healing power. We want to be enabled to be the best disciples that we can be so that when we finally see him face to face, we can celebrate and dance with joy that in the name of Jesus, we were able—just like those first disciples—to bring down Satan and to tread on snakes and scorpions that still represent the evil in our world.[10]

By praying the Lord's Prayer, we learn how to use our faith to do Jesus' will in the world. When we open our eyes to the places that Jesus wants to go, when our hearts cry out in pain about the evil that we see, and when we then do something about it, we can bring down Satan and tread on snakes and scorpions. We don't have to be specially trained or gifted to be conquerors over the evils that exist in our world. We do have to be faithful.

We must also open our eyes and our hearts to find the allies that we will need to make a difference in this world, just like Rev. Angel Sullivan discovered when she traveled to the Republic of Georgia. When we do, we'll find people who also love God and who want to do good in the world. We'll find people who we know are God's people, even though they don't live like we live and may not even believe as we believe. The world is full of good people who want to join in the effort to bring more of God's goodness into those places where goodness is needed. It's our job to work with all people who desire to help bring God's kingdom on earth. It's God's job to judge all of us.

When we pray the Lord's Prayer, if we want this prayer to be answered, we must be like those faithful disciples and commit our hearts, our souls, and our minds to doing the work that God wants done in this world. We are to live out our revolutionary faith tenaciously, in spite of any obstacles we may face. We are to live like we really mean what we are praying for—like we truly want what we are asking for in this powerful prayer to happen.

Only then will the prayer have the deep meaning and power that Jesus offers to enlighten us and strengthen our work as disciples. Only then can we find God's answer to our prayers. Only then will we truly become the ones who change the flavor of the world and illumine it, as the salt and light that Jesus expects us to be. Only then will Christianity as it exists today be revolutionized into a powerful force for change that will make the world a better place for all, just as Jesus always intended.

Deepen

The United States is not only one of the most powerful nations in the world; it is a highly Christian country. A 2011 poll showed that the U.S. had the highest population of Christians in the world, over 246 million.[11] The number has dropped over the years, yet the United States continues to have a majority of Christian citizens; slightly more than 70 percent of U.S. Americans identified themselves as Christian in 2014.[12] The Lord's Prayer is intended to help lead those who follow Christ to a deeper commitment of faith and give them greater power to do God's work in the world. Imagine the powerful impact this number of Christians could have on our society by following Jesus' teachings with the power that he offers.

The United States is also plagued with deep societal problems that seem to be impenetrable to all efforts to resolve them, including the highest incarceration rate of any country in the world; a growing, staggering gap between the rich and the poor; entrenched poverty and all of the ills that come with it; an increase in both labor and sex trafficking, which includes children; a proliferation of gun violence; and racial animosity that continually shows up in racism, racial profiling, racial disparities, and racial discord. There is much kingdom-building work yet to be done in this country and in our world!

For this Deepen session, we'll consider the Joint Declaration of Religious Leaders Against Modern Slavery, signed
in 2014 by Christian leaders (Catholic, Anglican, Orthodox,
and Lay-Christian) as well as leaders of Buddhist, Hindu,
Jewish, and Muslim (Sunni and Shia) faiths.[13]

Rev. Sullivan's story and that of the Joint Declaration of
Global Religious Leaders are two examples of how very different people of faith can come together on common ground,
and the good that can come out of our joining together with
different people for a common cause. World change can only

We, the undersigned, are gathered here today for a historical initiative to inspire spiritual and practical action by all global faiths
and people of good will everywhere to eradicate modern slavery across
the world by 2020 and for all time.

In the eyes of God each human being is a free person, whether
girl, boy, woman or man, and is destined to exist for the good of all in
equality and fraternity. Modern slavery, in terms of human trafficking, forced labor and prostitution, organ trafficking, and any relationship that fails to respect the fundamental conviction that all
people are equal and have the same freedom and dignity, is a crime
against humanity.

We pledge ourselves here today to do all in our power, within our
faith communities and beyond, to work together for the freedom of all
those who are enslaved and trafficked so that their future may be
restored. Today we have the opportunity, awareness, wisdom, innovation and technology to achieve this human and moral imperative.

happen if we are open to going to all of the places that God wants us to go, just like those first disciples, and discovering the power that we wield together with others who want God's will to be done in the world.

Here is the printed text of the Joint Declaration for easier reading:

"We, the undersigned, are gathered here today for a historic initiative to inspire spiritual and practical action by all global faiths and people of good will everywhere to eradicate modern slavery across the world by 2020 and for all time.

In the eyes of God each human being is a free person, whether girl, boy, woman or man, and is destined to exist for the good of all in equality and fraternity. Modern slavery, in terms of human trafficking, forced labor and prostitution, organ trafficking, and any relationship that fails to respect the fundamental conviction that all people are equal and have the same freedom and dignity, is a crime against humanity.

We pledge ourselves here today to do all in our power, within our faith communities and beyond, to work together for the freedom of all those who are enslaved and trafficked so that their future may be restored. Today we have the opportunity, awareness, wisdom, innovation and technology to achieve this human and moral imperative."

This powerful document was signed by Pope Francis; Her Holiness Mata Amritanandamayi (Amma); Venerable Bhikkhuni Thich Nu Chan Khong (representing Zen Master Thích Nhất Hanh); The Most Ven. Datuk K Sri Dhammaratana, Chief High Priest of Malaysia; Rabbi Dr. Abraham Skorka; Rabbi Dr. David Rosen; Dr. Abbas Abdalla Abbas Soliman, the Undersecretary of State of Al Azhar Alsharif (representing Mohamed Ahmed El-Tayeb, Grand Imam of Al-Azhar); Grand Ayatollah Mohammad Taqi al-Modarresi; Sheikh Naziyah Razzaq Jaafar, the special advisor of Grand Ayatollah (representing Grand Ayatollah Sheikh Basheer Hussain al Najafi); Sheikh Omar Abboud; the Most Reverend and Right

Honorable Justin Welby, Archbishop of Canterbury; and His Eminence Metropolitan Emmanuel of France (representing His All-Holiness Ecumenical Patriarch Bartholomew).

INDIVIDUAL DEEPENING EXERCISES

1. Read Luke chapter 9. Focus on what Jesus is teaching and showing the disciples. What things do the disciples get right? Where do they fall short? Take some time to think about your own Christian walk and what you may need to improve on as a follower of Christ.

2. Meditate on what it means to be a Christian in the United States. What do you believe should be the Christian response to the societal concerns about human trafficking in the Deepen section above? Do some research on how others in your church or in your local community are involved in helping to fix the problem.

3. Where can you go, either in the United States or somewhere else, where you will find people whose culture is very different from your own? How would you feel about being in the midst of them? How might you learn more about them, and how might you reach out to get to know them better?

4. How does the Joint Declaration of Religious Leaders Against Modern Slavery exemplify the hope of people of faith coming together to truly make a difference in the world?

GROUP DISCUSSION

1. Review the chapter.

(a) Why do *you* think the disciples asked Jesus to teach them to pray?

(b) What kind of power were the disciples seeking by learning to pray like Jesus?

(c) Many Christians have been taught to repeat the words of the Lord's Prayer by memory, and we routinely recite it together in public worship. How often do we really think about what the words mean? How might we engage this prayer, individually and corporately, in more meaningful ways?

(d) What does the author mean: "Jesus' words speak many volumes"?

(e) What does it mean to "live like we really mean what we are praying for"?

(f) Discuss your thoughts about working with people of different cultures and faiths to accomplish God's will.

2. Read aloud Luke 9:1-6, 10:1-12, and 10:17-24 and discuss the following questions.

(a) How might these adventures have helped to shape the disciples' understanding of the words that Jesus taught them to pray?

(b) What does it mean today to go out without a purse or bag or sandals?

(c) What are the things that Jesus wanted the disciples to do when they interacted with the people they met?

(d) What kind of demons do people face today that Jesus would want us to cast out?

3. Review the Deepen section.

(a) Discuss what you think must have been involved to get the leaders of global religions around the world to come together to pledge to achieve the "moral imperative" of stopping modern slavery.

(b) How is this Joint Declaration a modern kind of "going out to every town and place where he himself intended to go," as Jesus sent the disciples?

(c) Do you think that working together with people of other
faiths to challenge human trafficking is the right thing to
do? Why or why not?

Closing Prayer

Form a circle and pray together. Begin by slowly and expres-
sively reciting the familiar words of the Lord's Prayer. Then,
taking turns, pray for the will, the wisdom, and the power to
be faithful followers of Christ by implementing the words of
this prayer in your life.

NOTES

1. R. Alan Culpepper, "The Gospel of Luke," in vol. IX of *The
New Interpreter's Bible*, ed. Leander E. Keck, et al. (Nashville:
Abingdon Press, 1995), 233.

2. From Wikipedia: "Today 83.4 percent of the population [of
the Republic of Georgia] practices Eastern Orthodox Christianity,
with the majority of these adhering to the national Georgian Orthodox Church. . . . Religious minorities of Georgia include Muslims (10.7 percent), Armenian Christians (2.9 percent) and Roman
Catholics (0.5 percent). 0.7 percent of those recorded in the 2014
census declared themselves to be adherents of other religions. . . ."
See https://en.wikipedia.org/wiki/Georgia_%28country%29.

3. Luke 6:17, 20: "[Jesus] came down with them and stood on
a level place, with a great crowd of his disciples and a great multi-
tude of people from all Judea, Jerusalem, and the coast of Tyre and
Sidon. . . . Then he looked up at his disciples and said: 'Blessed are
you who are poor, for yours is the kingdom of God.'"

4. See Matthew 16:13-16: "Now when Jesus came into the district of Caesarea Philippi, he asked his disciples, 'Who do people
say that the Son of Man is?' And they said, 'Some say John the
Baptist, but others Elijah, and still others Jeremiah or one of the
prophets.' He said to them, 'But who do you say that I am?' Simon
Peter answered, 'You are the Messiah, the Son of the living God.'"
We do know, however that Judas at some point decided to betray
Jesus (Luke 22:1-5) and that the disciples denied Jesus after he was
arrested (see Mark 14:48-50, 66-72). However, none of this took
place before the disciples asked Jesus to teach them to pray.

5. See Luke 9:43b-46: "While everyone was amazed at all that he was doing, he said to his disciples, 'Let these words sink into your ears: The Son of Man is going to be betrayed into human hands.' But they did not understand this saying; its meaning was concealed from them, so that they could not perceive it. And they were afraid to ask him about this saying. An argument arose among them as to which one of them was the greatest."

6. See, for example, Luke 5:10b-11: "Then Jesus said to Simon, 'Do not be afraid; from now on you will be catching people.' When they had brought their boats to shore, they left everything and followed him." See also Luke 5:27-28: "After this [Jesus] went out and saw a tax collector named Levi, sitting at the tax booth; and he said to him, 'Follow me.' And he got up, left everything and followed him." (Levi is later referred to as the disciple Matthew.)

7. Luke 12:22-23 and following: "Therefore I tell you, do not worry about your life, what you will eat, or about your body, what you will wear. For life is more than food, and the body more than clothing."

8. One example is in Mark 7:27, when Jesus says to the Syrophoenician woman who asks him to heal her daughter: "Let the children be fed first, for it is not fair to take the children's food and throw it to the dogs." How many people have struggled with what sounds to us like Jesus calling this non-Jewish woman a dog? I think Jesus was speaking to this woman on a different level, a level that only she could understand. Jesus knew something in her history that only she knew, likely relating to the historically contentious relationship between Phoenicians and Jews. She understood the point he was making and responded accordingly.

9. John 14:12: "Very truly, I tell you, the one who believes in me will also do the works that I do and, in fact, will do greater works than these, because I am going to the Father."

10. Luke 10:17-19, 21: "The seventy returned with joy, saying, 'Lord, in your name even the demons submit to us!' He said to them, 'I watched Satan fall from heaven like a flash of lightning. See, I have given you authority to tread on snakes and scorpions, and over all the power of the enemy; and nothing will hurt you.' . . . At that same hour Jesus rejoiced in the Holy Spirit and said, 'I thank you Father, Lord of heaven and earth, because you have hidden these things from the wise and the intelligent and have revealed them to infants. . . .'"

11. According to a chart posted on the Pew Research Center website, dated December 19, 2011, the United States had the largest number of Christians among the countries of the world, estimated in 2010 to be 246,790,000. Brazil had the second largest with 175,770,000 Christians, followed by Mexico with 107,780,000. See http://www.pewforum.org/2011/12/19/table-christian-population-in-numbers-by-country/.

12. The Pew Research Center website also included a 2014 poll that showed that between 2007 and 2014, the percentage of adults who described themselves as Christians fell from 78.4 percent to 70.6 percent. See http://www.pewforum.org/2015/05/12/americas-changing-religious-landscape/.

13. See http://www.globalfreedomnetwork.org.

Chapter 2
Three Teachings

In Luke's Gospel, after Jesus taught the disciples the words to pray, he also taught them through parables. These parables were designed to help the disciples understand the power they would receive from their heartfelt prayers to God.

We now look at these teachings before studying the prayer to help guide our understanding of, and deepen our thoughts about, what we're praying for when we pray the Lord's Prayer. Jesus taught them that the Holy Spirit would guide them. That's what happened to Jeanne Allert, as will see in the opening story for this chapter. She was moved in her heart to reach out to God's people who were in great need. When she turned her focus to helping others, she found that her spirit was also fed. At the end of this chapter, we will close with some statistics that show us the work that God has assigned to believers in our time.

Life in Our Time

Jeanne Allert was a corporate success, traveling to share her technical knowledge of the Internet at business conferences across the globe. That changed about ten years ago, when her broken heart made her do a 180-degree turnaround. It all started after she met a group of church folks who took her to one of the poorest streets in an impoverished neighborhood in Baltimore, Maryland, where they prayed with and for women who walked that street to meet the quotas their pimps set for them. The church group offered the women food, prayer, and a way out.

At a church-sponsored carnival on that street, Jeanne met one girl, Heather. Frail and addicted to prescription drugs, Heather said, "I'm thirsty," when Jeanne asked her if she needed help. Jeanne gave her a drink, some food, and her time, and she listened to the girl's story of how she went from being a happy, normal child to an adolescent sex slave. Her mother's former boyfriend had kept in touch with her after breaking up with her mother. When she turned fourteen, he persuaded her to run away from home, and then he trafficked her along the I-95 highway corridor. After hearing Heather's story, Jeanne asked her, "What do you need?" Heather responded, "Underwear." Jeanne's heart broke. "I just couldn't understand how this could happen in the United States," she said.

After parting ways, Jeanne couldn't let Heather go from her heart. She bought underwear and drove to that street time and time again, until one day she found her. She gave her the gift, and Heather was gratefully surprised that Jeanne remembered her. After this, a Scripture passage haunted Jeanne and ultimately called her to further involvement. It was the words of Jesus in Luke 12:48: "To whom much has been given, much will be required." This was the beginning of Jeanne's amazing journey to becoming the founder of The Samaritan Women, a national Christian organization that provides transitional and restorative shelter programs for women recovering from domestic human trafficking, with an emphasis on life-rebuilding, personal accomplishments, social reentry, and spiritual reconciliation. One of their goals is to "inspire people—inside and outside of the Church—to engage in combatting domestic human trafficking through awareness, prevention, service, and advocacy."

At the time of this writing, in a quiet, peaceful, retreat-like location, the Samaritan Women now offers three houses and can care for up to forty women per year rescued from sex slavery. They have served more than sixty women since they opened in 2011. Jeanne marvels at where all this has taken her: "It just seemed like everything I had done in the corporate life was preparing me for the work that God had for me."[1]

The lessons that Jesus taught in Luke 11:5-13 were intended to help the disciples understand what to expect from God when they prayed the prayer that he taught.

The Midnight Call for Help

"Suppose one of you has a friend, and you go to him at midnight and say to him, 'Friend, lend me three loaves of bread; for a friend of mine has arrived, and I have nothing to set before him.' And he answers from within, 'Do not bother me; the door has already been locked, and my children are with me in bed; I cannot get up and give you anything.' I tell you, even though he will not get up and give him anything because he is his friend, at least because of his persistence he will get up and give him whatever he needs."

To drive home the power of praying, Jesus asked his disciples to imagine that they knocked on the door of a friend with a request for food to feed an unexpected guest, but the friend said, "Go away. Don't bother me." The disciples would have understood clearly that no real friend would do such a thing. Such behavior was unimaginable in their day and culture because of the great importance of hospitality in their society, engrained in biblical tradition from Moses' time: "The alien who resides with you shall be to you as the citizen among you; you shall love the alien as yourself; for you were aliens in the land of Egypt" (Leviticus 19:34).[2]

Jesus emphasized this teaching by pointing out that even if the friend wouldn't respond to the request out of friendship, he would respond because not getting up would be a violation of the stringent hospitality code of the culture. Jesus' point was that even if the sleeping man weren't that great of a friend, he would eventually respond to the persistent knocker because it was simply the honorable thing to do.

Jesus wanted the disciples to understand that if they could expect a not-so-good friend to respond to a knock on the door in the middle of the night out of a moral obligation to do so, they could surely expect God, who is holy and loving and worthy of praise, to respond to their prayers. Remember that Jesus was talking to faithful disciples who wanted most of all to do God's will. Jesus wanted them then, and he wants us today, to know that God will always respond to the prayers of faithful disciples. Not because God has an obligation to do so, like the not-so-good friend, but simply because God will respond faithfully to those who want to do God's will. Jesus knows how important it is for us to understand that God will hear and respond to our prayers.

I expect that most people who pray to God have at some time found themselves wondering whether God really has paid attention to their prayers. At times I have questioned what seemed to be God's lack of response to my prayers, only to discover that the answer was there—later than I expected or in a different way than I expected. There are lots of prayers out there for which people are still looking for answers. Jesus' story helps us all to see that when we don't seem to get a response from God, the problem is not that God is not paying attention—the problem is either in our unwillingness to wait for God's response or in our inability to understand or accept God's response. In the next two teachings, Jesus helps us to understand without a doubt that God will respond, and what kind of response we should expect.

Asking and Receiving

"So I say to you, Ask, and it will be given you; search, and you will find; knock, and the door will be opened for you. For everyone who asks receives, and everyone who searches finds, and for everyone who knocks, the door will be opened" (Luke 11:9-10).

How many times have these verses been cited without reference to the Lord's Prayer? If we take them out of the literal context, then we hear Jesus saying that God will give everybody everything they pray for. It is very dangerous to understand this passage that way!

Too many people have been told that if they faithfully and sincerely pray, God will give them anything they want. When people who are taught this don't receive what they've prayed for, they become confused, thinking something is wrong with them or their faith—or worse, they think something is wrong with God. We need to understand clearly that Jesus was speaking to his disciples, who were his students, and Jesus already knew that what they wanted was to be the best disciples they could be for God. He knew that what they sought was the power to do God's will in the world. They were not being taught that they had the power to control God through their prayers. Nothing could be further from the truth!

John 15 helps us to understand this teaching as it applies to sincere disciples. Jesus was talking to his disciples during his last supper with them before he headed to the cross. He declared: "I am the true vine, and my Father is the vinegrower. . . . Abide in me as I abide in you. Just as the branch cannot bear fruit by itself unless it abides in the vine, neither can you unless you abide in me. . . . If you abide in me, and my words abide in you, ask for whatever you wish, and it will be done for you. My Father is glorified by this, that you bear much fruit and become my disciples" (John 15:1, 4, 7-8).

In this chapter of the Gospel of John, Jesus committed twice to giving the disciples anything they asked for. Jesus told them that he is the vine and if they remain in him, they are like branches on his vine. The way to remain on his vine is by obeying his commandments. He then reminded them of the new commandment he has given them—to love each other as he has loved them. Then in verse 16 Jesus repeated the promise he made in verse 7: "You did not choose me but I chose you. And I appointed you to go and bear fruit, fruit that will last, so that the Father will give you whatever you ask him in my name."

Jesus' offer to give the disciples whatever they asked in his name is clearly explained in the metaphor of the vine and branches. The disciples must be working to yield the kind of fruit that Jesus, as the vine, will produce. The disciples would have known that a single vine can only produce one kind of fruit; the branches on the vine can only produce the same kind of fruit that the vine produces. Again, we must understand: Jesus knew that the disciples wanted to be empowered to more effectively do his will in the world. His offer to give them anything they asked for applies to this desire, and only if they remain on his vine—if they obey his commands and stay committed to doing his will in the world. Then they will be enabled to produce wonderful fruits—to do "great works"—in his name.

Jesus wants all of his disciples to stay connected to him in order to produce the fruits of discipleship. These fruits are defined by what he sent them out to do while he was in the world—to share the good news that the kingdom of God has come near by bringing love, healing, and wholeness in Jesus' name. Our hearts are to desire this more than anything else. The fruits we desire to produce are to be consistent with what he has taught and commanded us, with the highest commandments to love God and love others. God's willingness to give us whatever we ask for is inextricably tied to whether we have a strong, heartfelt desire to go out as faithful disciples to do the work that God wants us to do in this world, which is all to be driven by our love for God, for one another in the body of Christ, and for others in our communities and world.

We are to understand that Jesus teaches us to pray the Lord's Prayer so that we might be better empowered to do the work we are called to do as his disciples. With this as our desire, we are to be persistent and bold in our requests, and God will hear us and provide us with everything that we need. We may not even know ourselves what are our needs, but God certainly knows. Our job is to ask, like those faithful disciples, for God to supply our needs so that we can do God's will, and then to faithfully wait for the answer, trusting that God will hear us and provide us with everything that we need. In the next teaching, Jesus tells us exactly what we will receive.

The Good Parent

"Is there anyone among you who, if your child asks for a fish, will give a snake instead of a fish? Or if the child asks for an egg, will give a scorpion? If you then, who are evil, know how to give good gifts to your children, how much more will the heavenly Father give the Holy Spirit to those who ask him!" (Luke 11:11-13).

In this illustration, Jesus helped the disciples to see that, just as they always try to give their children what is good, God does the same for them—and even more. We must understand that God will never give us anything that will harm us. The key to understanding what God will give us, and the key to all of these teachings, is in the last line of this illustration—to those who pray to do God's will in the world, God will give the Holy Spirit. The Holy Spirit is the good gift that will provide the power we need to be the best disciples we can be.

In the Gospel of John, Jesus tells us that if we truly love him and do what he has commanded then God will give us the Holy Spirit to be with us forever (John 14:15-18). Jesus let the disciples know that even though he would no longer be in the world, he had not left them, and he has not left us, as orphans, because the Holy Spirit will dwell in us. The Holy Spirit, the Counselor, will guide us in truth. The Holy Spirit will tell us what is yet to come, and will bring glory to Jesus by helping us understand the messages that God has for us (John 16:13-15). Jesus prayed to God for us, asking that we would be one with each other and that we would be one with God and with Jesus by the Holy Spirit (John 17:20-23).

In John 7:37-39, on the last day of the Festival of Booths, Jesus stood and said that anyone who believes in him would quench their thirst with the living water that he would provide, and which would then flow from them like "rivers of living water." The text explains that this "living water" is indeed the Holy Spirit, to be received by all who come to believe in Jesus. We are to understand that the Holy Spirit is Jesus' gift to us, will be provided in answer to our prayers, will be with us, and, if we do what Jesus has commanded us to do, will be unleashed into the world through us. How amazing is that!

The Holy Spirit is all that we need to be empowered to do God's will in the world. We need nothing more. If we are persistent in our prayers to God to be better disciples, and live like we mean what we pray, then Jesus says God will bless us—not with everything and anything we ask for, but with the power of the Holy Spirit, which is absolutely better than anything we could ask for. With the Holy Spirit working in our lives, all those things we need and all kinds of things that we don't even know how to pray for are provided to empower us to do God's will.

It is important to understand that the presence of the Holy Spirit in us is not some magical, other-worldly experience that takes over us and causes us to do things that we have no control over. The Holy Spirit is not a ghost! The Spirit does have power, but it is the power to help us navigate through life in ways that are consistent with Christ's teachings. The Holy Spirit has power that we cannot control, but does not control us. We receive the Holy Spirit only as much as our hearts are open to the experience.

I think most people feel some level of the presence of the Holy Spirit in worship, like when the people sing together, abandoning all worries and concerns, with hearts and minds focused together on God. When God's people sing heartfelt praises, something special happens, bringing joy and peace and power to the gathering. Or when the preaching speaks not just words, but truth that moves our hearts, and we feel and know that God's grace and mercy is with us and will lead and guide us, drawing us to respond with heartfelt "Amens." Or when the prayers of the people reflect our shared longings, our pain, our gratefulness and love for God, bringing uncontrolled tears to our eyes and shouts of joy from our lips.

The power of the Holy Spirit is available to each of us individually, through our heartfelt desire to serve God in ways that are consistent with God's desires for us. We feel God's presence through the Holy Spirit, not as an overwhelming force, but in different ways. Maybe we feel it as a gentle touch, as a still, small voice, or as a thought that brings unexpected understanding. Perhaps we feel it as a desire to shout "Hallelujah!" and "Glory!" for the things that God has done. The Holy Spirit is God's presence with us, to which different people respond in different ways, and even with one person the Spirit is not always felt the same way.

When we dedicate our hearts to God's will and God's way, we find the Holy Spirit tugging on our conscience, encouraging us to do the right thing, no matter how tough that might seem. We find ourselves having strength beyond our believed ability to hold on, no matter how difficult the path may be. We find ourselves with courage that we didn't think we had, or sharing mercy that we thought we couldn't, saying the right words when we didn't know what to say, and forgiving even when it just seemed too hard.

With the Holy Spirit, we find ourselves more capable of seeing others with the boundless mercy and love that Jesus has for them. We find ourselves like Rev. Sullivan, finding God in people who do not share our cultural traditions. We find ourselves seeking to find the good that is in people who are different from us, especially those who are born on the edges of life, which includes being born into poor and difficult circumstances as well as rich and overly indulged circumstances. With the Holy Spirit guiding us, we find our hearts crying out against evil and injustice in this world, and committing ourselves to work against it, like Jeanne Allert. The Holy Spirit guides us not to judge or condemn, but to love and to want to help others.

The presence of the Holy Spirit leads us in the right way, gently guiding our hearts and minds and wills toward the forgiving and loving ways of Jesus. This is the power that we have, and it is power that goes beyond worldly under-standing, empowering us to do more than we can expect or even think to ask for. This is the power that we are to use to make a difference in the world. It begins with our willingness to allow God to take us to places where we may not have ever thought to go, like Rev. Sullivan going to the Republic of Georgia, and Jeanne Allert going into a poverty-stricken, broken-down street in Baltimore.

The apostle Paul sums it up for us in the doxology he provides in Ephesians 3:20-21: "Now to him who by the power at work within us is able to accomplish abundantly far more than all we can ask or imagine, to him be glory in the church and in Christ Jesus to all generations, forever and ever. Amen." Paul lets us know that through the power of the

Holy Spirit that is at work in us, the same power that we are to pour out into the world, Christianity can truly become a revolutionary power for good in the world.

These teachings help us know that God will answer our faithful prayers to be the best disciples we can be by pouring out to us the awesome power of the Holy Spirit, who will help us to become the powerful force in the world that God expects us to be. With this understanding and guidance, we'll go back to look at what Jesus says we ought to specifically ask for when we pray.

Deepen

The following information about poverty in the United States is from *Hunger Notes*, an online publication of the World Hunger Education Service (WHES) (citations omitted). The official poverty measure is published by the United States Census Bureau and shows that, in the United States:

- In 2015 there were 43.1 million people in poverty. This is down from 46.7 million in 2014, which was near the largest number in the 52 years for which poverty statistics have been published.

- The 2015 poverty rate was 13.5 percent, down 1.2 percentage points from 2014. However, the 2015 poverty rate was 1.0 percentage point higher than in 2007, the year before the most recent recession. (The poverty rate was at 22.4 percent in 1959, the first year for poverty estimates.)

- The 2015 poverty rate for blacks was 24.1 (down from 26.2 percent in 2014), for Hispanics 21.4 (down from 23.6 percent in 2014), and for Asians 11.4 percent (not statistically different from 2014). For non-Hispanic whites the poverty rate was 9.1 percent.

- The poverty rate for children under 18 was 19.7 percent in 2015, down from 21.1 percent in 2014. The number of children in poverty was 14.5 million, down from

15.5 million. Children represented 23.1 percent of the total population and 33.6 percent of people in poverty.

- 19.4 million Americans live in extreme poverty. This means their family's cash income is less than half of the poverty line, or about $10,000 a year for a family of four. They represented 6.1 percent of all people and 45.1 percent of those in poverty.[3]

INDIVIDUAL DEEPENING EXERCISES

1. Imagine you are sitting at Jesus' feet, with a strong, heartfelt desire to strengthen your faith and to make a difference in the world for him. Take your time and read carefully, then meditate on, Jesus' words in John 15:14-17. What parts speak to your heart? Why?

2. Read Revelation 3:14-22. Jesus is displeased with the church in Laodicea, telling them that because they are only "lukewarm" he is about to spit them out of his mouth. This church is in a wealthy city that was widely known for its banking establishments, medical school, and textile industry.[4] The church felt that it was rich and had become self-satisfied, but Jesus described them as "wretched, pitiful, poor, blind, and naked." Jesus counsels the church: "Buy from me gold refined by fire so that you may be rich; and white robes to clothe you and to keep the shame of your nakedness from being seen; and salve to anoint your eyes so that you may see." Jesus is asking them to seek from him what is needed to get right with God, which means repenting from their self-satisfied, lukewarm approach to being a church.

(a) Reflect on how easy it is to become self-satisfied when you are in a comfortable place. Consider whether you and/or your church may be at risk of becoming self-satisfied in a lukewarm faith because you have gotten used to being comfortable.

(b) Think about what Jesus meant when he told the church in verse 20: "Listen! I am standing at the door, knocking; if you hear my voice and open the door, I will come in to you and eat with you, and you with me." We often understand this to mean that Jesus is knocking on the hearts of unbelievers and sinners to be let in, but Jesus was talking to the church, which already thought Jesus was there with them!

3. There are all kinds of resources available to let us know that poverty is well entrenched in the United States, one of the richest countries in the world. How do you feel when you read about this kind of poverty? Do you feel worried, helpless, detached, concerned, or something else? How do you think Jesus would react to the high level of poverty in such a rich nation?

4. Consider what motivated Jeanne Allert to become involved in the effort against human trafficking. Is there anything that moves your heart like hers was moved? What might you do to follow your heart?

GROUP DISCUSSION

1. Review the chapter.

(a) Why is understanding the historical context of the hospitality code important to understanding the "Midnight Call for Help"? Discuss how this teaching might apply to all Christians, keeping in mind the biblical context: Jesus was talking to his dedicated disciples and had just taught them how to pray.

(b) Ask if any of the group members were taught that, if we pray sincerely enough and have faith, God will give us what we ask for—especially when what we're asking for is something that we believe should be pleasing to God, like bringing someone out of an addiction or bringing someone into faith. What are some positive and negative outcomes of this belief?

(c) The author states: "With this as our desire, we are to be persistent and bold in our requests, and God will hear us and provide us with everything that we need." What is the desire referred to here? How does John 15 help us to understand this?

(d) Discuss how you understand these statements: "The Holy Spirit is all that we need to be empowered to do God's will in the world. We need nothing more."

2. Read aloud Revelation 3:14-22. What was Jesus displeased about? What does Jesus mean when he tells the church he is knocking? Discuss how Jesus' knocking on the door of the church in Laodicea relates to Jesus' telling us in Luke 11:9 to knock so that he can open the door to us in response to our prayers. Which knocking must come first?

3. Discuss your feelings about poverty from Individual Deepening Exercise #3.

4. Discuss whether you believe that Jesus is knocking on the door of our North American churches, seeking to be let in. Assuming that he is knocking, discuss what we will need to do to let him in.

NOTES

1. Read more: http://thesamaritanwomen.org.

2. "In ancient Israel, hospitality was not merely a question of good manners, but a moral institution which grew out of the harsh desert and nomadic existence led by the people of Israel. The biblical customs of welcoming the weary traveler and of receiving the stranger in one's midst was the matrix out of which hospitality and all its tributary aspects developed into a highly esteemed virtue in Jewish tradition. Biblical law specifically sanctified hospitality

toward the *ger* ('stranger') who was to be made particularly wel-
come 'for you were strangers in a strange land'. . . ." See http://www
.jewishvirtuallibrary.org/hospitality.

3. See http://www.worldhunger.org/articles/Learn/us_hunger_facts
.htm.

4. "Laodicea (near modern Denizli) was the wealthiest city in
Phrygia during Roman times and the head of the 'circuit' of 'the
seven churches in the province of Asia.' The city lay on one of the
great Asian trade routes, and this ensured its commercial prosperity. Laodicea was a leading banking center. . . . The Lycus Valley
produced a glossy black wool, the source of black cloaks and car-
pets, for which the city was renowned. Laodicea was also the home
of a medical school and the manufacture of collyrium, a famous eye
salve." *NIV Archaeological Study Bible* (Grand Rapids: Zondervan, 2005), 2052 fn. 3:14-22.

Chapter 3
"Father, hallowed be your name"

The opening line of the prayer that Jesus taught helps us to focus on our relationship to God. All who believe in Christ are children of a most holy God who deserves our praise and worship. We will examine the two parts of this opening separately, because each tells us something different and important about how we are to relate to God.

Jesus teaches his disciples in this prayer and by his own example that we are to participate in the faith community, gathering on a regular basis to worship together. The church is the family of faith through whom God's will is to be accomplished in the world.

For some believers, however, the church experience has just not been attractive, and there are many believers in our time who feel that attending church is not necessary. Rachel Sloan shares her opinion about one such group. Her article "What Millennials Don't Want from the Church"introduces this chapter.[1]

Other believers have had negative church experiences. Jennifer Maggio is one of these people. Her church experience as a child caused her to leave the church and made it difficult for her to return. We will wrestle with her story as part of our deepening exercise at the end of this chapter.

Life in Our Time

What Millennials Don't Want from the Church

By Rachel Sloan

Life as a Millennial is hard. My iPhone is over a year old and does not have Siri. The Internet at my apartment is pretty slow. My Apple laptop is HUGE and does not have retina display. My iPad doesn't have enough free space for the new Coldplay album.

But the most frustrating part of being a Millennial is that my church does not understand me.

Churches often think in this vein:

1) We need more young people in the church.

2) How do we get more young people in the church?

3) We need a room in the church where we can install flashy lights and smoke machines.

4) We need to find a praise band.

If we build it they will come, right? Maybe not.

Despite [Millennials'] love for technology and social media, churches cannot simply slap a contemporary service together, create a Facebook page and call it quits, and then blame us when we do not show up.

Millennials (despite the terrible things you are told to believe about us) want real, authentic worship and real, authentic churches. We want churches that want to have a relationship with us.

We do not want churches to immediately advertise to us how great their contemporary service is, how amazing their young adult Sunday school class is, how sizable their group of young adults is, as if to say: "Of course we want you here! Just stay in your niche where we cannot see you and have fun over there while the rest of us run the church and make the big decisions."

We do not want you to immediately shove us off to a part of the church where we will never be seen or heard from again. If churches want Millennials to walk through their doors and stay there, they need to learn how to fully incorporate us and our ideas.

Whatever your church does well, there is a faction of Millennials that wants to be a part of it. Is your church passionate about social justice, worship or ministry to the local community? Do that, focus on that and Millennials may end up at your church.

Then let us help you do that. We do not only want to attend church on Sunday morning. Many of us care and want to be involved in a church; we just have not found ones that will let us in.

We are not going to a church that does not care about our ideas and we are not going to a church that is not willing to fully embrace us. Would you?[2]

"Father"

Jesus first teaches us to address God as "Father" when we pray. He tells us to use the familiar Aramaic term "Abba" for Father—like "Papa"—not normally used to address God in the Jewish tradition.[3] Jesus used this name for God because of his special relationship with God. By teaching us to call God "Abba," Jesus is letting us know that we, too, have the right to claim a special relationship with God.

For Jesus to tell us to call God "Abba" is absolutely empowering! Romans 8:15 tells us that we can call God "Abba" because we have received the spirit of "adoption," in other words, the privileged position of having the full legal standing of an adopted heir in Roman culture. We are enabled to pray boldly to our Heavenly Parent because we know that through Jesus we are offered God's presence and God's favor. Because God is love, we know that the love God has for us is unconditional, and it is wider and deeper than we can ever imagine. By teaching his disciples to call God "Abba," Jesus helps us understand that we are the beloved children of God, joint heirs with Jesus to God's kingdom.

As mentioned in the last chapter, in John 17:20-26, Jesus prays to Abba, asking that all who will come to believe in him (as Messiah) may become one with Jesus the Son and with God the Father: "As you, Father, are in me and I am in you, may they also be in us, so that the world may believe that you have sent me."

Then Jesus prays the most amazing thing: "The glory that you have given me I have given them, so that they may be one, as we are one, I in them and you in me, that they may become completely one, so that the world may know that you have sent me and have loved them even as you have loved me" (verses 22-23). How amazing! Jesus prays that all who come to believe in him will be glorified and will be united with God the Father, the Son, and the Holy Spirit. Our special relationship with God includes having our hearts and minds in sync not only with other believers, but also with the Triune God's plans for us.

Jesus prays for us to be brought into complete unity with one another "so that" the world will come to know that Jesus is truly the Son of God, and so that all will learn that God loves the whole world. Letting the whole world know about God's love through Jesus Christ is what is most important for our discussion here. The "so that" tells us that we have been given the inheritance of Christ, not only to save us from the sting of death, not only to give us the privilege of being full heirs and beloved children of God, but also to live our lives with clear purpose. That purpose is to share with the world through our words and our work the truth that Jesus is the Son of God who loves the whole world. When we do that, we are living in unity with God, and that means we are living in unity with God's purpose for our lives and with God's vision for the world. When we live in that unity, the power of the Holy Spirit is God's good gift to us.

Jesus Set the Example

Jesus set the example for how we are to live like we truly believe God is our "Abba" by showing us how to live in right relationship with our Heavenly Parent. Jesus prayed to God often. I imagine in those conversations with God he sought direction, strength, and courage to complete God's will. Jesus' prayer in the Garden of Gethsemane is one of the few times when the Bible reports the *words* that Jesus prayed. In that heartfelt, agonizing prayer, Jesus recognized that the job before him was too much for the flesh. So he asked Abba that God's will, not his, be done. That is the example that we are to follow.

Living Like We Mean It

To live like we accept the inheritance Jesus has given us, the right to call God "Abba," is to live faithfully, as children of God, trusting that God loves us and that what God wants for us is best. We know even when we go through difficult times that our Abba in heaven is lovingly watching over us. We call to God for help when we need it, knowing that God will not fail us. We do our best to please God, who has done so much to help us.

When we claim God as our Abba, we are constantly aware that we are God's children with a purpose to accomplish in this world. We recognize, like Jesus, that all that we are and all that we have been given are for this purpose, which is both our desire and our joy of living. We offer our lives back to Abba by using our gifts and talents to honor God and to accomplish God's purposes, no matter what position we may hold or where we may be located in this world.

Just like Jesus in Gethsemane, as children of Abba, we openly accept that God's will is what must be done. God's will is what we are to accept, and God's will is what we must do; it defines both how we live our lives and our purpose to accomplish in life. We must trust that God, our Father, wants nothing but what is best for us, no matter how difficult our course in life may be. We pray often to continually search for the will of God in all circumstances that we face.

No matter how hard we try, we will fail sometimes because the flesh is weak. We must understand that all that we can do is try our best, and even then, sometimes we will fall short in our efforts to do God's will. But with sincere and heartfelt prayer, God's grace will always be shared with us. We learn to accept the loving grace of God, our Abba, who will help us by sending the power of the Holy Spirit as promised. We learn further that with our continued sincere prayer and dogged persistence, we are able to rise above our failures and to accomplish amazing and wonderful things, just like those seventy-two (or so) disciples who returned to Jesus after being sent out with nothing but their faith.

Understanding that God is our Abba helps us to know we are the beloved children of God, who offers to us bountiful blessings. As 1 Peter 2:9 tells us, "[we] are a chosen race, a royal priesthood, a holy nation, God's own people, in order that [we] may proclaim the mighty acts of him who called [us] out of darkness into his marvelous light."

"Hallowed be your name"

The instruction to boldly call God "Abba" is immediately followed by a humbling reminder of who Abba God is: "Hallowed be your name." We are permitted to go to the throne of grace, calling God "Abba" with confidence, but in our approach to God we bow down, humbly recognizing that this gift of inheritance is more than we will ever have a right to deserve, because God's name, God's being, God's essence, is supremely holy.

Jesus has given us this opening line of the prayer to help us recognize and remember our proper relationship with God.

We are to understand that as children of God, even though we are honored as heirs with Jesus, we are still only human. We will make mistakes. We still find ourselves fearful. We can only try in our own broken ways to accomplish God's purposes because we can only see life as though we're looking through a dark glass. The best that we can offer can never be enough to pay for the gift to be heirs to God's kingdom, which Jesus has claimed for us.

I don't believe this first line of the prayer is so much a petition, as some have suggested.[4] It is instead an opening address that acknowledges both our closeness to God and our separateness from God. We are empowered as the beloved children of God, yet we must bow down to give God the glory that God deserves from all of creation. We must acknowledge both of these contrasting levels of our relationship with God first thing when we pray, lest we forget who we are and to whom we are speaking.

Being allowed to call God "Abba" must be always linked in our minds to the fact that we don't deserve such an honor. We must always remember that God's great grace and mercy, God's boundless love for us, and God's continuing presence in our lives are initiated by God, and not by anything that we could do to earn them. We must approach God with humbleness, and we must know that this humbleness is what we are to share with others in the world. We have no basis to claim self-righteousness; we can claim some of God's righteousness only if we obey God's commands to share God's grace and mercy, boundless love, and supportive presence with others who are in need. We have no right to look down on or judge anyone, ever. Calling God both "Papa" and "Most Holy" defines for us the blessed and humble character we must own if we are to go out in the world in Jesus' name to do God's will.

Acknowledging that God's name is holy also helps us to recognize that all of God's creation is beautiful and should reflect the goodness of God. As honored children of God, we are to seek to increase God's goodness in the world so that others will come to know just who God truly is.[5] So we honor God, we worship God, we say to God, "You are most holy," out of a complete sense of gratefulness that we have been called and empowered as God's favored children, and out of a complete sense of humbleness, knowing that we don't deserve the position that we now have a right to claim. We bow down to God in humble faithfulness that God is real, that Jesus is the Christ, and that the Holy Spirit is with us to comfort and empower us as we journey through life with a mission to accomplish for God: bringing God's goodness into the world so that others may know just who is the God we serve.[6]

Jesus Set the Example

Jesus set the example for us on how to live our lives as if we truly believe that God is most holy. In addition to praying to God often, Jesus worshipped God with the people. He honored the religious rituals of his time. While he was often critical of the religious leaders of his time, he did not dismiss the religious traditions. He went to the synagogues. He participated in the temple worship and the holy days. He challenged what he knew to be wrong thinking and wrong practices by the religious leaders.

He saw the people of faith as his brothers and sisters, a family of faith called to serve God, who is both his and our Father: "For whoever does the will of my Father in heaven is my brother and sister and mother" (Matthew 12:50). His desire was for the people of faith to properly honor God.[7] His goal was to help bring the family of faith to deeper understandings of what their faith meant. In his Sermon on the Mount he said he had not come to abolish or change the laws of his people, but to fulfill them (Matthew 5:17). His desire was, and still is, to deepen his followers' understanding of the religious writings and laws. He loved the people of faith, the holy writings, and the religious rituals; he wants us to use them all in ways that better reflect the love of God.

Living Like We Mean It

To live like we believe that our Abba's name is holy is to actively engage with the community of faith. We are to follow Jesus' example and gather regularly with other believers to worship together. We are to gather with other people of faith, because we all claim the same loving "Abba." We bow down in communal prayer before the holiness of God with our brothers and sisters in Christ. We participate in the gathered believing community to deepen our understanding of God's Word and to work together as one body in Christ, sharing our gifts of tithes, time, and talents. We are to be faithful to the church because the church is God's plan for accomplishing God's will on earth. We are to be one in the Spirit with our brothers and sisters, brought together by our belief in Jesus and by our loving Abba, who is worthy of our praise.

Congregational worship is not optional for Christ's disciples. Yet there is no one way to correctly worship God, except "in spirit and in truth."[8] That means no matter what the worship format, our worship of God must be guided by our sincere belief that God is worthy to be worshipped. We don't worship God out of habit, but out of love. We don't truly worship God by dutifully repeating memorized words that have no real meaning to us. We don't worship God because that is what "good" people do. We go to church to please no one but God. The purpose of the gathering is to join with other believers to worship God simply and solely because God deserves to be worshipped.

I have heard many people claim to be "spiritual but not religious," and I recognize that this growing trend of so-called Nones (no religious affiliation) and Dones (abandoning the religious affiliation of the past) comes from a widespread distrust of and disillusionment with the institutional church. Yet

I believe passionately that being part of a family of faith is vital to our life as disciples of Christ. Such a family challenges us to learn from and grow through our relationships with other children of God—those who will see God a little differently, experience the world distinctly, and invite us to expand our understanding of who we are in relation to God, "our Father," and to our siblings in Christ. The gathered community of faith can provide new insights to deepen our faith as well as good role models and friends who will join us on our spiritual walks. And I truly believe there is a church community for everyone who believes and really wants to worship God with a family of faith.

The best part about worship is that when the faithful gather to praise God in spirit and in truth, God shows up in the praise and the prayers. The Spirit of God, the *Shekina*—the power of God's presence that provides healing, helps us to gain deeper understanding, and provides us with unquenchable hope—moves through the congregation and is felt deeply. There is no feeling like it that this world can offer.

If you've never felt moved in your heart among the gathering of believers, I suggest you explore other churches. Look for a church where your spirit is fed, where you mind is engaged, and where you feel connected to people who want to actively work for the kingdom. When you find that church, you will not be just a "church-goer." You will feel the amazing power of the Holy Spirit in the worship, and that power is yours to take out into the world to serve as a disciple of Christ. And you will also find others who will join you in your kingdom-building work. Jesus didn't send the disciples out alone; he sent them out two by two, to support each other.

After sharing your faith in the world, you will want to return again and again to worship God in the community of believers, relating your accomplishments and sharing the joy of knowing you have received power in Jesus' name to cast out demons in the world. When you experience that power, you will know that you are part of the revolution that God is calling for, and your desire will be to truly praise God with all of your being. Being entitled to call God "Abba" is absolutely empowering!

Deepen

Here is Jennifer Maggio's story, posted on www.iBelieve.com on July 18, 2013.

Why I Stopped Going to Church

By Jennifer Maggio

I grew up in the Deep South in the middle of the Bible belt. Going to church was a way of life for us. We went to church every Sunday and most Wednesdays. And almost everyone I knew did the same. Interestingly, however, my parents rarely went with me. From the time I can remember, I was driven to the front door of the church and dropped off, then picked up after services were done. As I grew older, this made me very uncomfortable. All of my friends had their parents with them. *Why couldn't mine just come to church, too?!*

One Sunday, the pastor delivered a message on families and the importance of staying strong, staying in the Word, and supporting one another. He wanted to pray over families and invited us all to the front of the church to spread across the altar and stage for prayer time together, as a family. My twin sister and I, who were only about ten at the time, slowly walked forward. We sat next to each other and watched as other families—real families, complete families—prayed with each other. We sat alone, embarrassed. I could not wait for service to be over so that I could bolt out the front door. I am certain I was every shade of red, as I hurriedly rushed to my father's car.

I finally mustered up the courage to ask him why he never attended church. He explained that after my mother died, he swore he would never go back to church. (My mother was killed by a drunk driver on a Sunday morning while driving to church.) He insisted, however, that it was very important for me to go. I walked away from that conversation confused, hurt, and angry.

Over the next several years, I continued to attend church without my father, but after having two children outside marriage, I, too, fell away. My excuses were many:

The church is full of hypocrites.
I don't fit in. There's no one else like me.
I have a close relationship with God and don't need church.
I study the Bible on my own at home.
The church will judge me.

The longer I stayed away from church, the easier it was for me to continue to do so. And the truth is, my journey back into God's house was a long, hard one. It was only after examining my life at a very dark and lonely time that I made the decision to return. Even then, the urge to withdraw was strong. I convinced myself that I did not fit in, no one understood, and others would judge.[9]

INDIVIDUAL DEEPENING EXERCISES

1. Read John 17:20-26. Think about what it means to be one with God the Father and God the Son through the power of the Holy Spirit working inside of you. Meditate on how this should make a difference in how you live.

2. In our world, it is natural to admire those who are rich, famous, and powerful. We read the headline stories about them, gather around them, seek their favors, and consider it a blessing to get an autograph or some personal acknowledgement that we have been in their presence. God is the creator and owner of all that we know, God's power is unlimited, and God is pretty famous, too! By being given the right to call God "Abba," we have been gifted with a close personal relationship as beloved children to one who has greater wealth, power, and fame than all of those humans we adore. Yet when we gather to worship God at church, we often are hard-pressed to find the kind of excitement we feel when we are in the presence of a popular rock star, a great sports hero, a beloved president, or a billionaire business tycoon. Think about whether you feel your close relationship with such a mighty God is something to be really excited about. If you feel that your worship gatherings should be more exciting, how can you help to make that happen?

3. The next time you go to church, pay close attention to everything you see, hear, and feel when you enter the doors: the worship space, the interactions among the members and friends who are gathered there, the music, the prayers, the sermon, the activities after worship, etc. What is it that attracts you to this church? If you had never been to this church before, would you come back? Why or why not? How can you help to make it more exciting?

4. Consider Jennifer Maggio's story. If that were your church, how might you have reached out to her? What could you have done when she stopped coming to church? Think about who in your present church may need your encouragement now, and how you might help them.

GROUP DISCUSSION

1. Review the chapter.

(a) Discuss the different levels of intimacy you feel with these four ways of addressing God: God, Sovereign, Father (or Mother), Papa (or Mama).

(b) Why does the author say it is "absolutely empowering" to be entitled to call God "Abba"?

(c) Discuss the connection between calling God "Abba" and then saying to God, "Hallowed be your name." How do we live like we believe that God is our Abba and that God's name is supremely holy?

2. Some people have difficulty with the concept of God as father because God is neither male nor female, which is true.[10] But Jesus calls God "Father," and our right to do so comes by inheritance through Jesus. Yet we also know that the manifestation of the Holy Spirit in both Hebrew and Aramaic (Jesus' spoken language) is a feminine word (Shekina), as is the Spirit of God (Ruach). The wisdom of God is characterized as female in the Hebrew Bible, and as well by Jesus: "Nevertheless, wisdom is vindicated by all her children." (Luke 7:35).

(a) Read Proverbs 8:1-11.

(b) If God does not have a gender, why do you think we have traditionally chosen to use male images and language for God, and not female? Discuss how we can honor God both as our mother and our father, while acknowledging that God is not to be limited by either of these intrinsically human depictions.

3. Take a few minutes to share some thoughts from Individual Deepening Exercise #3.

4. Discuss what the author means: "To live like we believe that our Abba's name is holy is to actively engage with the community of faith." Share with each other why you believe attending church regularly is or is not important. What kind of things might you do to make coming to church more inviting to "spiritual but not religious" people? What kind of things might you do to help people like Jennifer Maggio feel welcomed at church?

5. What do you think Rachel Sloan means when she says Millennials want "real, authentic worship and real, authentic churches"? Do you agree or disagree with her assessment? Why? How do you believe your church fits within her analysis? Discuss some things your church might do to become more inviting to Millennials.

NOTES

1. The Pew Research Center defines Millennials as the generation born after 1980. The oldest group of Millennials in 2016 would be in their mid-30s about the time of this publishing. See http://www.pewsocialtrends.org/article/millennials-in-adulthood/sdt-next-america-03-07-2014-0-06/.

2. See https://baptistnews.com/2013/10/23/what-millennials-don-t-want-from-the-church/#.WPDgd_KrJil. ©2013 Baptist News Global. All rights reserved.

3. For example, M. Eugene Boring tells us that "In the first century both Jews and Greeks commonly addressed God as 'Father.' The common synagogue invocation was 'Our Father, our King'. . . . It was characteristic of Jesus to pray to God simply as *abba* . . . [which] is not only a child's term of endearment, like *Papa*, *Mama*, and *Dada*, but was also used by adult children in addressing their fathers." M. Eugene Boring, "The Gospel of Matthew," in vol. VIII of *The New Interpreter's Bible*, ed. Leander E. Keck, et al. (Nashville: Abingdon Press, 1995), 203.

4. See, for example, R.T. Kendall, *The Lord's Prayer: Insight and Inspiration to Draw You Closer to Him* (Grand Rapids: Baker Publishing Group, 2010), 75: "This is the first petition of the Lord's Prayer: 'Hallowed be your name,' a petition designed that God will be put in His rightful place by our worship. . . . Another way of putting it: The Lord's Prayer is given to teach us primarily to seek God's face, not His hand."

5. N. T. Wright suggests that in addition to acknowledging the holiness of God, the phrase "hallowed be your name" is a petition seeking for God's glory and righteousness to be recognized by the whole world: "Our Father in heaven, may your name be honoured. That is, may you be worshipped by your whole creation; may the whole cosmos resound with your praise; may the whole world be freed from injustice, disfigurement, sin, and death, and *may your name be hallowed*." N. T. Wright, *The Lord and His Prayer* (Grand Rapids: William B. Eerdmans Publishing Company, 1996), 22.

6. Philip Mathias has a similar approach to what this part of the prayer means: "Hallowing God's name is not just a formula of words or a wholesome internal psychology. 'Father, hallowed be thy name' calls for deeds, even politics. It calls upon us to happily distribute our talents to all God the Father's children without favor, and to recognize and share their gifts without a hierarchy of values. It calls on us to support the poor and liberate those of God the Father's children who are oppressed." Philip Mathias, *The Perfect Prayer: Search for the Kingdom through the Lord's Prayer* (Minneapolis: Augsburg Books, 2005), 70.

7. See Mark 11:15-17, where Jesus drove the money changers out of the temple in Jerusalem, saying, "Is it not written, 'My house shall be called a house of prayer for all nations?' But you have made it a den of robbers."

8. John 4:24: "God is spirit, and those who worship him must worship in spirit and truth."

9. Read more: http://www.ibelieve.com/faith/why-i-didn-t-go-to -church.html.

10. See Numbers 23:19: "God is not a human being, that he should lie, or a mortal, that he should change his mind."

Chapter 4
"Your kingdom come"

The kingdom of God is certainly a place where God's peace, love, and goodness reign. Regardless of whether you believe this world will ever reflect God's kingdom, you will likely agree that life on earth can sometimes be far from it. Poverty is one of the earthly qualities of life that can make life more like hell, as the statistics in Chapter 2 indicate. Poverty is destructive in itself, but when added to America's history of racism and racial discrimination, poverty's power to demean and destroy lives can be greatly amplified. Our opening story for this chapter helps us to understand how far from God's kingdom are the birth situations of many black people in our country and what this can mean for not only their lives, but also for our country.

Life in Our Time

Alton Sterling was a black man who was shot and killed while pinned to the ground by two white policemen on July 5, 2016, in Baton Rouge, Louisiana. His shooting started a new round of national protests against police aggression against black people, and also led to two mass shootings of police officers. On July 7, during a Dallas, Texas, protest of Sterling's death,

Micah Xavier Johnson fired ambush-style, killing five police officers and wounding seven other officers and two civilians; on July 17, Gavin Eugene Long shot and killed three police officers and wounded several others in Baton Rouge. He said he did it in response to Sterling's killing.

Alton Sterling's life typifies that of many African Americans who are unable to extricate themselves from the ravages of being born and raised in impoverished black neighborhoods in the United States. The following material is taken from two articles, a July 13, 2016, article in *The Washington Post*[1] and a July 6, 2016, article in the *New York Daily News*.[2]

According to *The Washington Post*, Sterling's mother died when he was fourteen years old, and his father by the time Sterling was nineteen.

"Alton pretty much raised himself," Quinyetta McMillon, the mother of Sterling's oldest son, said. . . . Sterling never graduated from high school. . . . He lived in a transitional housing program run by a local Baton Rouge church that houses other struggling men like Sterling—many of them formerly homeless, formerly incarcerated and black. There, Sterling paid $90 a week for a private bedroom. He cooked for fellow residents, biked to go fishing on the Mississippi River and took cans to the Triple S Food Mart. . . .

The *Post* further reports of Sterling:

[He] was in many ways the embodiment of an American—and particularly, a Louisianan—justice system that legal experts say is skewed heavily against black Americans. . . . At the time of his death at 37, Sterling had amassed a 46-page arrest record—with charges ranging from failing to wear a seat belt to burglary and domestic battery. . . . Each charge carried with it new and hefty fines as well as other requirements such as maintaining gainful employment, . . . [to] pursue a GED or trade school, pay $50 a month for his own supervision, pay

$200 for a special assessment at a high school, pay child support, perform community service, and attend the court's Effective Decision Making School.

Sterling's police record doesn't appear to reflect the opinion of some people who came to know him. The *Post* reported that his oldest son, Cameron Sterling, wanted everyone to know that his father was a "good man, no matter what anyone else has to say about him." The *New York Daily News* reported that while trying to make a living, Sterling sold CDs and DVDs in front of the Triple S Food Mart, where owner Abdullah Muflahi told the *Daily News* that "he didn't see Sterling get into confrontation, or pull out a gun." The *Daily News* further reported that Calvin Wilson, a resident at the Drop-In Center, told *The Advocate,* "I never saw him coming in here with a weapon, and I never saw him drunk. He wasn't a bad guy."

"I saw him every day," said Jaime Triplett, 36, who lives half a block from the Triple S. "He always kept a smile. He was the guy that when people came into the store disgruntled, the owner would say, 'Big A! Talk to your people.'" A friend and customer, Darian Gardner, told *The Advocate,* "He was nice. He wasn't a bad guy, he was respectable."

"Your kingdom come"

After acknowledging and affirming that we are children of a loving Abba who is most holy, Jesus teaches us to pray, "Your kingdom come." Some writers think of this part of the prayer as a petition for Jesus' return to come soon, which is a fine thing to pray for, but they do not believe it has further meaning.[3] Some believe that it is a request for God's kingdom to reside spiritually in individual hearts, which is another fine thing to pray for.[4] Others see it as a multifaceted petition acknowledging that God's kingdom-building work on earth is to be accomplished by believers.[5]

I agree mostly with this last point of view, but I don't see this part of the prayer as simply a petition. I believe that it is a confession of faith in the ultimate goal of Christian discipleship. When we say, "Your kingdom come," we're saying to God that we believe in the Lord's vision for this world and we want it to come to fruition. We're saying that we believe in the work that Jesus started when he was here, and we want to do our part to continue that work. This is why we are following Christ. We don't wait for God to do it alone; we confess to God that it is our desire to help make it happen.

Matthew's version of the Lord's Prayer unpacks this understanding by adding, "Your will be done, on earth as it is in heaven" (Matthew 6:10). This makes clear Jesus' desire for the disciples to continue the work he taught them. By starting the prayer with this heartfelt confession, the disciples open themselves to God's guidance in a very specific direction: how to build the kingdom of God—the place where God's will is done—on earth as it is in heaven.[6]

When Jesus sent the disciples out in Luke's Gospel, the good news that he gave them to share with the world as they brought healing and hope to the people was this: "The kingdom of God has come near." The disciples learned that they were to help bring the coming of God's kingdom because Jesus gave them the power to help make it happen. They had already experienced what it felt like to bring the kingdom's healing powers to the people, and they knew the great joy of accomplishing that work. More than anything else, they wanted to continue to show the world that, in the power of Jesus' name, the kingdom of God will drive out sickness and evil.

What does the kingdom of God look like? Jesus' example teaches us that the kingdom of God is where good news is preached to the poor, release is proclaimed to prisoners, the blind begin to see, and the oppressed are set free (Luke 4:14-21). Similarly, Jesus said that the proof of his being the Messiah is evident when "the blind receive their sight, the lame walk, the lepers are cleansed, the deaf hear, the dead are raised, and the poor have good news brought to them" (Matthew 11:2-5). That's what God's kingdom is to look like. Can't you see it? A place where all of God's beloved children feel the love of their Creator, where all benefit from the goodness of the earth that God created, where none are hungry or imprisoned, where none are blinded, where none are oppressed, and all are forgiven. Wouldn't you want to live in a world like that?

I suspect some of you are thinking: such a desire for the world has to be unrealistic, "starry-eyed" wishing. Such skepticism has no place in the minds of believers! "For nothing will be impossible with God" (Luke 1:37). Why are we so willing to give the world up to Satan, whom Jesus has thoroughly defeated? That's what we do when we think we have no part in bringing God's kingdom to earth.

Kingdom building begins when each one of us who dares to take the name "Christian" believes that Jesus was right about all that he taught, and that our job is simply to do our part to help make it happen. Kingdom building happens when kingdom-building believers work together to revolutionize the Christian faith to make it become the powerful force in the world that Jesus intended it to be. Kingdom building is accomplished when the world reflects the goodness of God.

The world is our challenge, given to us by God with the expectation that we are to do the "greater works" that Jesus has assigned to us. Our job is to heal the sick, tend to the needy, provide for the widows and orphans, bind the brokenhearted, usher in justice and righteousness, and so forth. We are to work together as God's empowered children to accomplish these purposes by serving others and by organizing and influencing the larger communities. And while the whole world is our challenge, we don't have to be concerned about whether what we do for God will be in itself world-changing;

we just have to believe that it's our job to do our part. We just have to figure out what our part is, then do it.

Our work is not limited to providing direct assistance to help meet the needs of those in our society who are suffering; our work includes working with others in society to change the unjust systems that keep suffering in place. God doesn't want us to just feed the hungry periodically while ignoring the systems that continue to make more and more people hungry. God wants us to have Christ-like, prophetic compassion to work on mending the broken systems that keep hunger, poverty, illness, war, and other evils so thoroughly entrenched in our world.[7]

Desiring for the kingdom of God to come on earth is a crucial element of the Lord's Prayer because without this desire, the kingdom-building work will not get done. It is a confession of faith that is required to be affirmed at the beginning of the prayer; without it, there is no purpose to be accomplished in the rest of the prayer. If we are to pray this prayer as Jesus teaches, we must be like the disciples who walked on earth with Jesus. We must truly believe that Jesus is the Messiah, and that God's kingdom is to come to earth through our faithful work as his disciples. If we do not deeply desire to do the work that God wants us to do on this earth—if we do not yearn in our hearts to be the best disciples that we can be for Christ—we will not be able to understand or receive the full power of this prayer. We simply will not become the salt and the light for the world that Jesus intended us to be as his followers.

Jesus Set the Example

Jesus set the example when he walked the earth. Although he looked at the world with his human eyes, he saw it through God's eyes. He looked at people with both boundless compassion and depths of understanding. He saw the hypocritical religious leaders for who they really were. He saw the needs of the poor and he saw the yearning of those who needed to be forgiven. Imagine how Jesus would have seen Alton Sterling, beginning from the time he was created in his mother's womb, with potential that was likely quashed by the circumstances of his birth. Jesus continually taught his followers in ways designed to help them see the people and the world around them like he saw them, so that they might understand the depth of the tasks required for kingdom building.[8]

An example of this type of teaching is the story of the good Samaritan, which Jesus told in Luke 10 to help people understand more fully the second great commandment, "Love your neighbor as yourself" (see Luke 10:25-37). The person who was left beaten on the road is not described in any way beyond his gender and his physical condition: he was simply a man who had been brutalized and was in trouble. No details were given about his race, culture, religion, or socioeconomic status. The victim represents all people who are in trouble on the road of life. Jesus depicted a Samaritan—looked down upon by the Jewish community and thought unfit for God's kingdom—as the person who exemplified love better than the religious leaders who crossed to the other side of the road in fear. In doing so, Jesus was letting his disciples know that God's view of righteous people is not limited by religion, culture, race, stature, or professed beliefs. God sees through all of our human qualifiers to look into the heart of each person and to see our needs, our shortcomings, and the measure of our love.[9]

Living Like We Mean It

When we sincerely pray, "Your kingdom come," with a desire to help make kingdom-coming happen, we will begin to see the world differently. As beloved children of God who want nothing more than to do God's will, we will try our best to see the world and all the people in it as their loving Creator sees them, even though we can only see as though we're looking through dark glass (see 1 Corinthians 13:12, KJV). We will try to see others through the eyes of Jesus, who was willing to forgive all of us even though we did not deserve it.

When we learn to see people as God sees them, our desire will be to help others, first and foremost. Our desire will be for others to see, hear, and feel the loving presence of God in their lives. Our desire will be to bring the justice and righteousness of God into the institutions of human life, to build the "beloved community" that is God's will.

The work we've been given is not easy to accomplish, and none of us can do it alone. But we are to understand that it is God's will for God's kingdom to come to earth, that it is our job to do our part to make it happen, and that God will send the Holy Spirit to help us accomplish this work, which is all that we need.

When we begin to really see and understand the world as God sees it with a desire to serve the people's needs, here are some things I believe will happen:

- We won't see color, race, ethnicity, or other distinguishing characteristics caused by the circumstances of birth as a reason to divide God's people into separate groups to categorize, rank, like, or dislike. We instead will see all as the beloved children of God, a beautiful rainbow of diversity designed according to God's amazing and loving creativity. We will recognize that we all are humans with more commonalities than differences, and we will understand that all people deserve our love simply because they are part of God's creation, our neighbors.

- We will no longer see different religions as necessarily antagonistic. Instead we will see people who are struggling in their own different ways and cultures to understand God. We'll work harder to find ways to relate and work together for the common good.

- We will understand that this earth and everything in it belongs to God, so we will no longer see people who come across our artificial boundaries as "illegal aliens" or "outsiders" trying to take away our jobs. We will instead see people who are desperately trying to make a living for themselves and to take care of their families. We will also see that there are abundant resources in the created world for all of us and, with some effort and mutual cross-border cooperation, those resources can be distributed so that all needs are met.

- Instead of seeing people with different political agendas as enemies or opponents because they don't want the same things we want, we will simply see people who have different views, some of which may be legitimate. These are people whom we must work with to make our society better for us all.

- Instead of seeing people who are poor as dependents who drain our resources because they are too lazy or don't know how to care for themselves, we will see poverty as the larger problem to address. We will realize our job is to figure out how to better share the abundant natural resources that God has provided for all of us, and to take care of the "least of these" who, because of their life circumstances, are unable to care for themselves.

- We will no longer see children hardened by the strife of impoverished communities as fodder for gangs, our prison systems, or to become sex slaves. Instead we will see them as children who themselves have been brutalized by their birth circumstances of struggle, strife, and abuse, with no one to help them through it. We will reach out to them in as many ways as we can to save them, for they are precious.

- We will know without a doubt that war and violence are not the answer to any of our differences, and we will join in the demand for peace.

- We will do everything we can to protect the earth, the good creation that God made and assigned to our care.

We must engage in kingdom building in all the ways necessary to make meaningful changes in the lives of the people we are to reach. It is good to feed the hungry, but the good news that the poor need to hear is that they don't have to be poor anymore. If kingdom building is our goal, then we must find ways to bring really good news to the poor, helping them in ways that enable them to have jobs, affordable housing, healthcare, and the ability to fix their own meals for their families in their own homes. We must find meaningful ways to make this beautiful world, which God created and put in our care, into a place where everyone can feel the love of their Creator. That's what kingdom building is.

There are myriad ways to participate in kingdom building. Kingdom building may mean working with others to build safe and affordable housing for the poor, finding new ways to make healthcare more affordable, becoming a "big brother or sister" for a child who needs it, petitioning local governments to provide harsher punishments for the "pimps" and "johns" who target vulnerable children in order to keep sex trafficking in place, providing safe shelters for children and women who are freed from sex slavery, meeting with local officials to address laws or law enforcement that is unfair or biased, petitioning governmental officials concerning laws and policies that are unfair, joining in peace marches and rallies, and so on.

Once we are clear on how we are to serve as children of God most holy, we will find that the Holy Spirit will empower us in ways we don't know how to ask for and can't even imagine. We will find the people we need to help us in our endeavors, we will find the words we need to say at the time we need to say them, we will find strength beyond our own capabilities to get us through our struggles, and we will feel God's presence guiding us in peace, joy, and love. This is how

God will answer our heartfelt prayers for God's kingdom to come on earth, which will make us a revolutionary power in Christianity and in the world.

The result for us will be lives filled with meaning and purpose, joy and fulfillment—truly abundant!

Deepen

Below is a list showing the ten states with the highest weekly church attendance, as of 2014.[10]

We might expect that Utah, Texas, Alabama, Arkansas, and Louisiana, being among the states with the highest weekly attendance rates, might better reflect the kingdom of Christ than some of the states with lower attendance rates. However, five of the states with the highest attendance in churches are

Top 10 States, Church Attendance

States with highest weekly attendance

	%
Utah	51
Mississippi	47
Alabama	46
Louisiana	46
Arkansas	45
South Carolina	42
Tennessee	42
Kentucky	41
North Carolina	40
Georgia	39
Texas	39
Oklahoma	39

Gallup Daily tracking
January–December 2014

among the ten states with the highest poverty rates: Alabama, Arkansas, Louisiana, Mississippi, and Tennessee.[11]

Six of these states also have very high incarceration rates: Texas has the highest number of residents incarcerated at 157,900 prisoners (a rate of 601 per 100,000 residents), and Louisiana has the highest rate of incarceration at 893 per 100,000 residents (41,246 prisoners). Mississippi, which is ranked second in weekly church attendance, ranks second in high poverty rates and also ranks second in sending people to prison: 21,426 prisoners at a rate of 650 per 100,000 residents.[12]

INDIVIDUAL DEEPENING EXERCISES

1. Read Luke 8:40-48, the story of the woman who had been considered unclean for twelve years because she could not stop bleeding, and how she was healed by touching the hem of Jesus' garment. Notice how Jesus treats her after she is healed. Then read John 8:1-11, the story of the woman brought to Jesus by the religious leaders because she had been caught in an adulterous relationship, who by law was to be stoned to death. Notice how gentle Jesus is with her. Imagine yourself in either of these women's positions. How does it feel to be healed and helped by Jesus? With the example of how Jesus dealt with these women in mind, pray to God about any of your personal concerns, with the knowledge that God loves you unconditionally and only wants what's best for you. Confess anything you feel a need to confess, asking for both healing and forgiveness.

2. Review the news articles about Alton Sterling. Pay close attention to his prior arrests and the reasons why he was arrested and fined. Think about Mr. Sterling as a beloved child of God. What do you think were the factors in his birth circumstances that brought him to the life he lived?

How might our social structure be enabled to better help people born into poverty? Remember how Jesus treated the woman found guilty of adultery who was to be stoned to death by law. How might Jesus see Alton Sterling? How does this kind of love and forgiveness reflect the coming of the kingdom?

3. Meditate on how you can help someone who might need healing or forgiveness. After meditating, try to pay closer attention to some of the people you frequently come into contact with and consider how you might better relate to their needs. Consider the needs of people you see on the streets who may be homeless, caught up in prostitution, or on drugs. How might Jesus' healing and forgiveness work through you for them?

GROUP DISCUSSION

1. Review the chapter.

(a) What does the author mean when she calls the petition "Your kingdom come" a "confession of faith in the ulti-mate goal of Christian discipleship" and when she says, "Desiring for the kingdom of God to come on earth is a crucial element of the Lord's Prayer"?

(b) Do you agree or disagree that God's kingdom coming to earth will help change it to a place where "all of God's beloved children feel the love of their Creator, where all benefit from the goodness of the earth that God created, where none are hungry or imprisoned, where none are blinded, where none are oppressed, and all are forgiv-en"? Why or why not?

(c) Discuss what the author means when she says we will "begin to see the world differently" when we sincerely pray this part of the prayer.

2. Read aloud Luke 10:25-37, the story of the good Samaritan, and then do some role-playing. Have someone in the group represent the religious leaders' viewpoint and justify their actions. Have someone represent the Samaritan's viewpoint, knowing that the person he was helping was an Israelite who likely would have looked down on him. Why did the Samaritan do it? Have someone represent the viewpoint of the innkeeper, and how he felt about what he learned in conversations with both the religious leaders and the Samaritan. Discuss how we justify leaving broken people on the road of life today.

3. Read Luke 4:14-21 aloud. Discuss your thoughts on whether a high level of church attendance in a state ought to make a difference in the state's poverty and incarceration rates. Why or why not? What might be some causes of both the high poverty and high incarceration rates in these states that the churches could address?

4. Discuss what you believe may be the reason the large population of Christians in our country has not become a more powerful witness to the kingdom of God and has not been able to ameliorate some of our long-standing societal problems like poverty, human trafficking, and mental illness.

NOTES

1. "Alton Sterling's Relatives Weather Scrutiny, Call for Justice," July 13, 2016. See https://www.washingtonpost.com/national/alton-sterlings-relatives-weather-scrutiny-call-for-justice/2016/07/13/dbf0ba60-490f-11e6-bdb9-701687974517_story.html.

2. "Who was Alton Sterling? What we know so far about the man killed by Baton Rouge Police," July 6, 2016. See http://www.nydailynews.com/news/national/alton-sterling-article-1.2700893.

3. See Oswald C. J. Hoffmann, *The Lord's Prayer* (San Francisco: Harper & Row, 1982), 32: "Let there be no misunderstanding about this. Jesus Christ did everything necessary to make the king-

dom of God come. He needed no help of any kind. The Kingdom needs no help today."

4. See R. T. Kendall, *The Lord's Prayer: Insight and Inspiration to Draw You Closer to Him* (Grand Rapids: Baker Publishing Group, 2010), 91: "Although the Kingdom of God can also be described in eschatological terms—meaning the Second Coming—Jesus clearly meant what is invisible, not what is visible. The kingdom of God takes place in the heart. . . . This is exactly what Jesus came to bring: the Most High God, who inhabits eternity, would live in the hearts of His people." Both Hoffman, (fn.3) and Kendall hold a position, popular in some religious circles, that God's kingdom comes into the lives of each of us when we accept Christ, and there is nothing further that we are to do relating to the kingdom. This theological perspective sees the world as holding many traps that can lead us away from God, and believes we are to resist these worldly temptations. This view sees God's kingdom taking place in each person's personal and spiritual life, with little or no responsibility to make the world a better place for all; the final fulfillment of God's kingdom will only happen when Jesus returns.

5. See Art Simon, *Rediscovering the Lord's Prayer* (Minneapolis: Augsburg Books, 2005), 52: "We are not powerless. God's way of answering many of our prayers is to give us the strength and wisdom to do what we need to do. We dare not give thanks for God's creation and proceed to despoil it. We cannot pray for employment but not go job hunting, pray for good government but not bother to vote, pray for good grades but not study, pray for hungry people but ignore opportunities to help them, or pray that people come to know Christ but keep our faith hidden."

6. See, for example, M. Eugene Boring, "The Gospel of Matthew," in Vol. VIII of *The New Interpreter's Bible,* ed. Leander E. Keck, et al. (Nashville: Abingdon Press, 1995), 203. Although Boring understands the opening petitions to be "primarily eschatological," he indicates that the phrase "your will be done, on earth as it is in heaven" adds an "impact on the present that calls for corresponding action."

7. See, for example, Isaiah 61:8: "For I the LORD love justice, I hate robbery and wrongdoing." See also Micah 6:8: "He has told you, O mortal, what is good; and what does the LORD require of you but to do justice, and to love kindness, and to walk humbly with your God?"

8. See, for example how Jesus dealt with the woman who was classified as "unclean" and who wanted to hide because she had violated the law in order to touch the hem of his garment and be healed (Matthew 5:25-34). He wouldn't let her sneak away without first healing her soul by calling her daughter and lifting her up so that her faith could be shown to the crowd.

9. Similar examples include the time when he blessed the Samaritan leper who was the only one of ten lepers to thank him for healing them (Luke 17:11-19) and his conversation with the Samaritan woman at the well, which violated many rules governing the behavior between Rabbis and both Samaritans and women (John 4).

10. This information was gathered by a Gallup poll between January 2, 2014, and December 30, 2014. It asked 177,030 American adults, aged 18 and older, how often they attended church, synagogue, or mosque: at least once a week, almost every week, about once a month, or seldom or never. We can safely assume that about 73% of those interviewed were Christians, so this poll can help us see which states have the highest number of Christians who attend religious services. See http://www.gallup.com/poll/181601 /frequent-church-attendance-highest-utah-lowest-vermont.aspx.

11. From the World Atlas website, November 26, 2015, based on the 2014 Census: http://www.worldatlas.com/articles/us-poverty -rate-by-state.html. Please note that data on poverty rates varies based on the different ways the rate can be measured.

12. See http://247wallst.com/special-report/2013/07/25/states -sending-the-most-people-to-prison/3/.

Chapter 5
"Give us each day our daily bread"

In a limited sense, this next petition focuses on our human need for food. We all need to eat to survive. But didn't Jesus teach that we are not to worry about where our next meal will come from, or what clothes we have, or where we live? Didn't he teach us not to worry about the material things of this world, and to not even worry about tomorrow (Matthew 6:25-34)? In this chapter we'll focus on this part of the prayer that Jesus taught closely, examining it from the point of view of disciples who were taught not to worry about themselves, but instead to concentrate on seeing to the needs of others. Our opening story helps us to see how this can work. It's about a group who prioritizes their mission of helping others through their restaurant business.

Life in Our Time

Sisters Of The Road is a nonprofit café in Portland's Old Town/Chinatown neighborhood, co-founded by Genny Nelson and Sandy Gooch in 1979. According to their mission statement,

"Sisters Of The Road exists to build authentic relationships and alleviate the hunger of isolation in an atmosphere of non-violence and gentle personalism that nurtures the whole individual, while seeking systemic solutions that reach the roots of homelessness and poverty to end them forever."[1]

This award-winning nonprofit has a unique approach to customers that focuses on welcoming everyone, respecting and treating all people with dignity, using a peaceful approach to deal with conflict, and continually advocating for the poor and the homeless. They offer low-cost meals (the most expensive item is $1.50) and use a barter system to allow people to work for their meals if they don't have cash. Their monthly activities include "Women's Care Day," "Community Care Nights," and "Food for Thought Forums." In 1985, Sisters Of The Road began a campaign to allow people to use food stamps to purchase prepared food in nonprofit dining facilities, which became a federal law in 1987. This amazingly loving and caring organization continually strives to honor the lives of all people, with a primary focus on maintaining the dignity of those who are poor and homeless.

Here's how one employee, Mary Kay McDermott, described what goes on at the café:

> As I looked around, I first spotted Sisters' African-American, tall, muscular, overly jovial, once-homeless, once-jailed cashier. He was taking orders patiently while making sure to check in with each customer about their current state of well-being as he always does. I remembered my first encounter with him—being a small town country girl from Iowa, I was more than a little timid talking to a black man who had been jailed and homeless not all that long ago.
>
> Next my eyes fell upon an elderly, mentally ill gentleman bussing the counter in front of me. Completely calm and collected, he did the job precisely as he had been taught. I recalled seeing him that morning outside the café, throwing awkward punches and angry words

at a person I could not see because he or she only existed inside the realms of his mental illness.

In the kitchen was where I caught my next image. There a trans woman dished up spaghetti plates for our hungry customers with an uncommon grace not usually seen in the kitchen where the staff is primarily male. With her hair in pigtails and a colorful, flowered apron she went about her work with a smile on her face and a hum on her lips.

That is when I heard a peculiar sound coming from the front of the café. I turned my attention in that direction only to catch sight of an obviously intoxicated clown creating balloon creatures for the customers he was waiting in line with. I had to shake my head, chuckle a little, and stop to think about where I work, where people find refuge from the insane streets and the even more wicked world. The cashier, mentally ill man, trans woman, and drunken clown may not have a place in the real world, but at Sisters Of The Road, they are welcomed. Not only are they welcomed, but their presence is accepted and appreciated.[2]

"Give us each day our daily bread"

This petition for daily bread has great depth. The request has been variously interpreted to mean that we have a right to pray to God for sustenance, that we need to stay aware of our daily dependence on God, that we should empathize with others who are needy,[3] and that "we may be fed with God himself."[4] These interpretations are of course solidly based. Yet the beauty of Jesus' words throughout the Gospels is that they often speak volumes more than we can fathom at any given time, and we can therefore continually mine them for deeper meanings.

To think a bit more about the meaning of this petition, we return to consider the disciples who asked Jesus to teach them to pray. In order to follow Jesus, they walked away from their support systems—their work, their families, their homes. They left behind all of their systems for daily sustenance so that they could wander around from place to place to learn from the Master Teacher. Jesus taught them not to worry about those things they left behind: "Therefore I tell you, do not worry about your life, what you will eat or what you will drink, or about your body, what you will wear. Is not life more than food, and the body more than clothing? . . . But strive first for the kingdom of God and his righteousness, and all these things will be given to you as well" (Matthew 6:25, 33). Jesus clearly wants his disciples to turn our thoughts away from what can too easily become our highest (and often our only) priorities—meeting our essential daily needs for food and shelter—so that we might become better at kingdom building.

So when the disciples asked him to teach them how to pray, Jesus taught them to ask God to provide their daily sustenance because followers of Jesus are given new priorities in life. This first petition is about learning to trust that God will care for those who are dedicated to doing God's will in the world. We must learn to trust God to take care of our basic needs, so that we can be freed to focus on the kingdom-building work that God wants us to hold as our highest priority. We are to commit ourselves to doing God's will in the world, no matter where we may be required to go or what we may be required to do. That commitment is to take priority over the mundane maintenance work of survival.

Jesus teaches us to pray for God to provide our daily bread so that we will always keep in mind that survival maintenance is secondary to the higher purpose to which God has called us. This petition requires that we turn the world's priorities upside down (or from God's perspective, right-side up again) in order to focus on what God wants from us. The world's priorities are put in proper perspective when we know that God's will is what is most important in the world, when we understand that God's kingdom requires us to focus more on the needs of others than ourselves, and when we learn how to live simply, not holding on to more than we need.

This does not mean that eating and sleeping are not important; they are obviously necessary if anything else is to be accomplished. But the primary focus of Christ's disciples is to serve God. Thus, this is a petition to help us to be clear about our priorities and more effective in our focus, and to learn to trust that God will provide. By praying to God to "give us each day our daily bread," we are essentially saying to God: "Because we are dedicating our lives to do your will in the world, we ask you to provide for our basic needs, so that we may be freed to better concentrate on the work you want us to accomplish."

Making sure that we have food and shelter so that we can survive is fundamental, of course, yet we must understand that the pursuit of meeting our own needs is not the only reason we exist. We are so much more than flesh! We can too easily find ourselves spending the majority of our lives focused primarily on what we eat, where we live, and what we wear. What starts out as the desire to meet our primary needs often ends up being the desire for more than we need, as we are constantly bombarded by commercials that make us think we need more and more, better and better, newer and newer, and bigger and bigger. Our pursuit of education, careers, and life choices all become centered on how proficient we can be in meeting these desires, which go far beyond our real needs.

When we unthinkingly go down this road, we progress from wanting more than we need to feeling that we have a right to have more. We really believe we deserve all that we can get, even if the only way we can get it is to max out our credit cards! Life can become a hollow pursuit of material abundance, where success is defined by how much more we are able to accumulate than others. Thus, we unthinkingly learn to worship wealth—*mammon*[5]—and find ourselves admiring wealthy people for no other reason than their wealth.

The life of abundance to which we have become accustomed can easily lead us to become like that rich man who asked Jesus how to get to heaven, but who wouldn't follow Jesus upon hearing that he must give all he had to the poor first (Matthew 19:16-24). From this lesson we understand that Jesus would have provided for all of the young man's needs, if only he had the necessary faith to relinquish his accumulation of stuff. God wants us to trust that God will provide for all of our true needs. This can be difficult for us when we're accustomed to having abundant material wealth. What is most disturbing is that good Christians with high personal morals seem to so easily get caught in this trap, not realizing there is something more for them to do with both their money and their faith.

Jesus Set the Example

Another of those few times that we overhear Jesus praying is found in John 17, when he prays to God for himself, his disciples, and all who will come to believe in him. One thing he says in the prayer for himself is that he has done his part, as he promised: "I glorified you on earth by finishing the work that you gave me to do" (verse 4). Jesus never strayed from the job that he came to accomplish. All that he did was to serve God. Everything. Jesus had the power to perform mighty miracles, but he never used that power to benefit himself. He healed the sick, cast out demons, mended broken hearts, fed thousands, controlled the wind and the waves, walked on water—each and every time, he did what he did to help others, never for himself. The work God had for him was primary; everything else was to support this primary purpose. And Jesus never took a job to meet his needs while serving God in his spare time.

Living Like We Mean It

To follow Jesus' example and live like we mean our request to God to "give us each day our daily bread" means to give our highest priority to the call to discipleship (see Jesus' challenge to the rich young ruler in Matthew 19:16-24). We must learn to live simply, knowing that there are more important and fulfilling goals in life than accumulating wealth. If we have a job, a place to live, and food to eat each day, God has already answered our prayer for daily bread. With this prayer answered, the question we must ask ourselves is, "Now what can I do for God?" A disciple's highest priority should always be building God's kingdom on earth.

Wouldn't it be wonderful if all Christians were so dedicated to the call to serve God? I don't mean that we all should try to be preachers or priests or to serve in some kind of paid religious position. If all of us who claim the title "Christian" would see our line of work as supplemental to our call to discipleship, each day we would find ways to use our positions as a means to God's greater end. Seeking to see the world through God's eyes, all of us as ambassadors of God would give priority to bringing love and healing and peace into the places we find ourselves, no matter what kind of job or position we hold to meet our basic needs.

Architects, engineers, and scientists would use their skills to find new ways of providing affordable housing for the poor and creating clean energy that is affordable to all and better for the earth. Lawyers would use their gifts to create legal systems that are fair and affordable so all could truly be treated equally under the law and justice would "roll down like a mighty stream" (see Amos 5:24). Chemists and scientists would work on cures for ailments that will help the broader world community, not based on how much profit could be made from selling drugs to the privileged few. Doctors would organize themselves to make sure that all people received healthcare at affordable prices. Governmental representatives would place a higher priority on building peace than on political agendas. Every disciple would work to live in peace and friendship with the people they work with, no matter what position they hold. That's sharing the good news.

We don't have to proselytize to bring God's reign into our workplaces. We don't even have to mention God's name. To be God's ambassadors in the world, what we have to do is see the people we work with through God's eyes and find ways to show that we love them, no matter who they are or how they might behave. We would work to bring peace and prosperity to all around us using whatever positions, gifts, and tools we have. We are to have that forgiving, loving, and nurturing presence that speaks Jesus to people who need to hear it without even mentioning Jesus' name. We are to focus on how we can make the piece of the world over which we have some influence better reflect the loving God whom we serve, trusting that God will provide what we need as we do God's work.

While we may not have to leave the comfort of home, job, and community to follow Christ, we must be open to the possibility that this is just what Christ wants us to do. God still calls people out from where they are to new adventures in life for Christ. If God is calling you, you'll know it. You will feel the pull to do something different from what you are doing or to go someplace you have never been before, like Rev. Sullivan in Chapter 1. If it is God's call to you, it won't let you continue with your life comfortably. Sometimes a disciple must be willing to step out on nothing but faith— leaving job, home, and security—to go to the better place to which God is calling him or her.

If you feel this kind of spiritual pull on your life, you will find people around you who are willing to help you and guide you to your new life in Christ. Talk to people in the church, your pastor, and others who have experienced the call in their lives. God will direct and lead you, and you won't regret it.

If we as Christians give priority to serving others wherever we may find ourselves working, like the owners of the Sisters Of The Road café, then the good news will be shared with others in a form that will feel real to them. People are more likely to be changed by a strong, loving, thoughtful, and kind presence than by intrusive, judgmental, and demanding proselytizing. Christians will gain respect and be seen as a people of wisdom. People will feel the presence of God through us, and they will be moved by it.

People will know that we are Christians by our love, and it all begins with asking God to provide for our needs so that we can live simply, trusting that God will provide for our daily needs so that we can keep our highest priority in mind at all times: bringing the kingdom of God on earth as it is in heaven. This is the priority system that will transform the world.

Deepen

This is an article posted by the United Methodist News Service (UMNS) on July 28, 2016, from Rushinga, Zimbabwe.

Church Brings Food Relief to Drought-Stricken Areas
By Taurai Emmanuel Maforo

Tashinga Chapatarongo, an 18-year-old pregnant mother, tied two 10-kilogram (22-pound) bags of meal on each side of her body and prepared for the long walk home.

She and about 300 others had come to the Rutuka United Methodist Church for food relief.

Chapatarongo said she had harvested a meagre 20-liter (22-gallon) bucket of maize at the close of the 2015–16 growing season because of drought in Zimbabwe.

"This is a miracle that has just happened and I am out of words. God bless this church," said Chapatarongo, who walked 10 kilometers, about 6 miles, from her home village of Muzeke to pick up the food relief. . . .

Churches in the Harare West District contributed 15 tons of maize and maize meal to the food bank launched earlier in the year by the Rev. Philip Musharu, the district superintendent, in response to the declared state of emergency due to the devastating effects of the drought.

The Rushinga food distribution was the initial step in assisting disadvantaged communities within the areas served by the district's churches.

"The drought has not only affected our harvest, but the water situation and livestock. Most boreholes in the Rushinga District have dried up and now many people have to drive their livestock for close to 10 kilometers (6 miles) to get water and the scarce pasture," said Wilson Jara, the Rushinga District social services officer. . . .

The United Nations Development Program reported in May that up to 4.5 million people, half of Zimbabwe's drought-stricken rural population, will need aid by next March as the agency seeks to plug a funding gap of $290 million for assistance.

The United Methodist Committee on Relief has worked in partnership with the U.N. World Food Program on food security needs in the Kariba District and Uzumba Maramba Pfungwe District, reported UMCOR's head of mission in Zimbabwe last spring.

The El Niño-induced drought has cut the output of the staple maize crop.[6]

INDIVIDUAL DEEPENING EXERCISES

1. When you watch TV, pay attention to the commercials and the things people are encouraged to buy. How many of those things do you really need? When you go into stores, pay attention to the many products for sale. Look at all the different brands and varieties of items like toothpaste, cereal, clothes, detergent, and toys. How many of those things do you really need?

2. Read Matthew 6:25-34. Spend some time thinking about how God has blessed you. If you are working, thank God for your job. If your physical needs are being met, thank God. If you have supportive family and friends, thank God.

If you have health and happiness, thank God. Look around you and thank God for all the material things you have gathered in your life. What can you do without?

3. As an example of what it means to "seek first the kingdom of God," the disciples gave up all of their security to follow Jesus, and discovered they had amazing power to bring hope and healing to others through the power of Jesus' name. How do Sisters Of The Road exemplify this kind of caring that reflects God's love for all people?

4. What might Jesus be calling you to do to bring hope and healing to others, whether in your present workplace or location or somewhere else? What might you be required to give up in order to do it?

5. Take some time to explore what your church denomination or your local church is doing to help others, particularly in poverty-stricken lands like some of the places in Africa. How do they involve members of the local churches in those places? How can you help?

GROUP DISCUSSION

1. Review the chapter.

(a) What does the author mean: "This first petition is about learning to trust that God will care for those who are dedicated to doing God's will in the world"?

(b) Discuss whether it would be easier to follow Christ in a place of great abundance or in a place of great poverty. What about in a place of great poverty in the midst of a place of great abundance?

(c) Discuss the author's conclusion: "People will know that we are Christians by our love, and it all begins with asking God to provide for our needs so that we can live simply, trusting that God will provide for our daily needs so that we can keep our highest priority in mind at all times: bringing the kingdom of God on earth as it is in heaven. This is the priority system that will transform the world." Do you think this is possible, or just wishful thinking? Why?

2. Read aloud Matthew 19:16-24, the story of "The Rich Young Man." Discuss why you believe the rich young man walked away sadly from Jesus. Do you think that Jesus' request to give all that the young man owned to the poor was too much to ask? Why or why not? What conclusions can you draw from this story about how we are to look at wealth today?

3. Discuss some ways that people who live in places of abundance can learn to live more simply. Imagine together what would happen if members of affluent congregations vowed to live more simply in order to help people who may be facing starvation, either at home or in other lands. What kind of help could they provide? How could they become personally involved in meeting the people who are in need? What kind of impact would their gifts make? How would they feel if they were successful in saving others' lives?

4. Try to identify some faith groups in your city, town, or neighborhood that are involved in working with local poverty, hunger, or homelessness, and bring the information to share with the study group. Discuss how the gathering of people of faith across denominational and cultural affiliations can make a difference in your communities as well as in poverty-stricken lands in other countries.

5. Discuss how the Sisters Of The Road's welcoming, non-judgmental, respectful, and generous approach to people who are homeless and impoverished makes a difference. How does their caring service to those in need, joined with their community organizing and advocacy, make their work more meaningful? Is their example one that can be duplicated on a mass scale? Why or why not?

NOTES

1. See http://sistersoftheroad.org.

2. Ibid.

3. See, e.g., William Powell Tuck, *The Lord's Prayer Today* (Macon, Georgia: Smith & Helwys, 2002), 54: "This petition begins with a reminder of our absolute dependence on God." Also at 59: "We cannot shut our eyes and ears to the sights and signs of malnourished bodies and the wailing cries of pain. Your prayer and my prayer for daily bread is directed to our Father, and we ask that he give us our daily bread. Our lives are intertwined with our fellow men and women around the world." See also Art Simon, *Rediscovering the Lord's Prayer* (Minneapolis: Augsburg Books, 2005), 64: "The prayer for daily bread is modest. It asks for enough. Not wants, but needs. Not too little, not too much. It is a prayer for contentment. Jesus warned people not to covet riches or worry about food and clothing. He knew that poor people were especially tempted to let worry grind them down; but he was far tougher on the affluent."

4. N. T. Wright, *The Lord and His Prayer* (Grand Rapids: William B. Eerdmans Publishing Company, 1996), 44: "The Kingdom-prayer isn't a prayer, such as some religions would advocate, for our desires to be taken away or annihilated. In bringing them into the prayer within the setting of the earlier petitions for God's honour, his kingdom and his will, it asks for our desires to be satisfied in God's way and in God's time. And, since God himself is most truly the deepest object of our hunger, this clause asks that we may be fed with God himself."

5. Matthew 6:24. *Mammon* is the Greek word for "property," often translated as "wealth."

6. See http://www.umc.org/news-and-media/church-brings-food-relief-to-drought-stricken-areas.

Chapter 6

"Forgive us our sins, for we also forgive everyone who sins against us"

Jesus phrased this petition of the prayer in such a way to emphasize that it is important for disciples to be willing to forgive. We are to forgive everyone. This radical teaching can be difficult for most people. Our opening story is about a church that was created to provide abundant forgiveness and support to people too often condemned by the world.

Life in Our Time

Rev. Will Shewey dreamed of starting a somewhat unusual church in Kingsport, Tennessee. As reported in the Holston Conference newsletter "The Call," Rev. Shewey was "so determined to begin a storefront ministry for forgotten people that he was willing to resign as a United Methodist pastor to make it happen." The article reports that in 2014, with the help of the conference, Rev. Shewey opened the doors of the church he named "Shades of Grace." "This will be an inclusive church," Shewey said. "None will be denied."

Shades of Grace provides a complex ministry to an inner-city community. Within a year, it moved from a fellowship hall in another church to its own location, with an average worship attendance of 160. "I had no idea we would be so steeped in the homeless population. I did not know the extent of the problem," Shewey said. Fifty to sixty percent of his congregation is homeless. Yet the church provides meals, showers, addiction help, GED education, job assistance, prayer, and friendship to a group of low- and no-income people throughout the week.

"They're completely different than any church I've ever seen," said Grady White, a Kingsport Police Department officer who sometimes worships and eats with the congregation. "They're actually willing to get their hands dirty when they're dealing with the homeless and other individuals that most people are not willing to work with," he said. "And they're right smack dab in the middle of where the homeless people are."

"This church is amazing. They don't judge," said Ally Kling, who came to Shades of Grace homeless and in distress. "They saw me on the side of the street with my bags, and they said, 'Come in. Come get dry. Eat.' And they prayed and prayed for me."

After only one year of existence, Shades of Grace became self-sustaining, including paying the pastor's salary, said the Rev. David Graves, Kingsport District superintendent. "Typically, that takes three years and hundreds of thousands of dollars of conference support," Graves said. As district superintendent, he has provided support to Shades of Grace by inspiring fifty-eight United Methodist congregations in the district to share both food and labor. Shades of Grace also caught the local media's attention, drumming up visibility and inspiring others to donate money, meals, mattresses, clothing, cots, and time.[1]

"Forgive us our sins, for we also forgive everyone who sins against us"

Matthew tells us that Jesus provided further instruction on the importance of forgiving others right after teaching the prayer: "For if you forgive other people when they sin against you, your heavenly Father will also forgive you. But if you do not forgive others their sins, your Father will not forgive your sins" (6:14-15, NIV). Forgiveness lives in the heart of Christianity, where disciples who want nothing more than to follow Christ must dwell. We are to live in forgiveness.

Learning to freely forgive others is another crucial component of effectively praying the Lord's Prayer because our willingness to forgive proves to the world that the greatest power of all is God's love. The depth and breadth of forgiveness that Jesus expects from us is increased dramatically by Jesus' teaching: "But I say to you that listen, Love your enemies, do good to those who hate you, bless those who curse you, pray for those who abuse you" (Luke 6:27-28). Rev. Dr. Martin Luther King Jr. preached on this text: "Far from being the pious injunction of a Utopian dreamer, the command to love one's enemy is an absolute necessity for our survival. Love even for enemies is the key to the solution of the problems of our world."[2]

Jesus knew that the disciples he taught would face powerful opposition to their part in God's plans.[3] That's why Jesus taught them to forgive everyone. This radical forgiveness carries with it great power to change hearts and save souls. Forgiving the wrongdoing of others, even our enemies, is key to helping the world understand true love, and when the world gets it, when the people in this world begin to understand that loving others is truly the right way to live, then the revolution will happen. Being willing to forgive as a way of proving the true power of love is the only way to bring the kingdom of heaven on earth. Forgiveness opens up the power of love to the world. Thus, forgiveness empowers Christian believers to become a mighty revolutionary force in the world.

We cannot truly love others if we are unable to truly forgive them.[4] If we are to interact in the world as disciples who represent a God who loved the world so much that he sent his Son to forgive us while we put him to an excruciating death on a cross, then we must have that same kind of extraordinary love. This kind of love goes beyond the bounds of normal human expectations and is proven by how willing we are to forgive. We may not have to die on a cross to prove our love for others, but we are absolutely required to forgive others as Jesus forgave us from that cross. To be a disciple of Christ is to be a forgiving person. There are no alternatives, no other options, no ways around this important part of the Lord's Prayer.

Three people who set the example on how to do this are Mahatma Gandhi, Rev. Dr. Martin Luther King Jr., and former South African President Nelson Mandela. They got it. They knew they could not be silent in the face of racism and oppression because to be silent would be to allow oppression to continue; to be silent would make them aiders and abettors of the evil; to be silent would not bring peace. So they fought, but they fought by harnessing the most powerful weapon in the world, using the love of God to lead their actions and their work. They greatly changed the dynamic of history and transformed the world by their powerful resistance to racism and oppression through active, nonviolent protest that did not threaten physical harm to others and that was always willing to forgive.

The kind of protest that will defeat the evil forces in this world does not stoop to using evil methods because it is based on the command to love. It's counterintuitive that the kind of rebellion derived from love and forgiveness is more powerful than evil, wrong, and oppression. This is possible only because God is love and God is all-powerful. We learn this lesson from Jesus' not only dying on the cross, but his being resurrected from the grave through the mighty power of God. Love is the most powerful weapon in this world, but we have to be brave enough to wield it, strong enough to be humble and loving, compassionate enough to be forgiving and kind, even when we are being hung up on the cross to die, even when we are in the crossfire of those who hate us, even when they want only to destroy us. No matter how powerful the evil forces we will face, we have to believe, to know without a doubt, that love will conquer all.[5]

Don't get me wrong. Sometimes people need to be held accountable for their wrongdoings. But they also need to be forgiven. As Christians, we are to be the first to forgive, because Christ has demanded this from us. If we don't forgive, we won't have the power we need to do God's will in this world, because we will have become too much like the world around us. We cannot be the salt and light in the world that we must be in order to build God's kingdom on earth if we do not learn to truly forgive others.

Forgiving others is important not only for those who are forgiven—it is important for the forgivers as well. When we are able to truly forgive, we build healthier relationships with others and we free our minds of negative baggage like hate, distrust, resentment, and anger. We cannot find the peace that Christ offers to us if we do not truly forgive others.

Jesus Set the Example

Jesus taught that loving others is one of the two greatest commandments, and that we are to love one another as he has loved us (Matthew 22:34-40; John 15:12). The profound example Jesus set for us on love is found in forgiveness, and sharing this lesson with us was his ultimate purpose in coming to live on earth as a human. The ten words Jesus shared while hanging naked and bleeding on the cross, painfully supported only by skewered hands and feet as he was publicly and cruelly mocked and scorned after being falsely accused, wrongly judged, and beaten overnight with extreme brutality—all the while holding the complete power to stop all of it with one word or possibly even just a thought—were: "Father, forgive them; for they know not what they do" (Luke 23:34, KJV). This godly example reaches deeply to move our hearts so that we might not only understand, but truly feel the great saving power of forgiveness that comes from uncompromising love.

Living Like We Mean It

Living out this petition is straightforward—but far from simple to implement. Our asking God to forgive us is tied to our willingness to forgive others. No matter how grave the injury or insult, we are to forgive, even if the recipient of our forgiveness does not ask for it, does not want it, and is not grateful. No matter how negatively someone else's behavior has affected our lives, we are to forgive with no expectation of a favorable response from them.

We are called to see every person as a beloved child of God, created to be a part of God's good creation. Those who do things to hurt and harm others have lost their way from God's plan for them. Many become lost because of difficult circumstances of their birth and early development environment, like we saw in Alton Sterling's story; others have mental problems; some have come under the influence of negative and evil thoughts over which they have no control; others have decidedly turned away from God. And there are some, likely many, whom we have simply misjudged.

Our job is to try to get back into right relationship with people whom we need to forgive and to bring them back into right relationship with God. We are to try to see people as God sees them, and as the songwriter put it, we are to "look beyond [their] faults and see [their] need."[6] Our job is to help them heal, to help them feel the loving presence of their Creator in their lives. It all starts with our willingness to forgive them.

Forgiving is not always easy; that's why it's in this prayer. There will be times when we need God's help to guide us into true forgiveness. No matter why people hurt others or do the wrong that they do, we are to struggle to see them all as God sees them, as beloved children of God who may be lost and who always have the potential of returning to the loving persons God created them to be. If possible, we are to help them find their way back through the combination of discipline, instruction, and loving forgiveness.

Just like we're often too willing to give the world over to Satan, I believe that we are often too willing to give other people over to Satan. We are willing to give up on people who commit heinous crimes. We are willing to give up on children who get involved with gangs and drugs or who become victims of sex trafficking. We look down on older prostitutes, who were most likely brought unwillingly into sex trafficking as children and have adapted to their situations by believing that life defines who they are, because they can see no other life for themselves. We find it easier to go to war with people who want to harm us than to do the tremendously difficult work of trying to reconcile our differences.

We also need to understand that to be forgiving does not mean that we allow evil and the destructiveness of hate and violence off the hook. We are not to allow ourselves to be brutalized, and we can't allow others to be brutalized. Jesus does not ask us to sacrifice our safety and security to those who would harm us. Jesus would not want anyone to live in an abusive situation. Nothing could be further from what his forgiveness on the cross means. We are beloved children of God, who wants only what is best for us, and while we are expected to forgive those who would harm us, we are not expected to live in a harmful situation. To be forgiving does not mean that we consent in any way to injustice and oppression for ourselves or for others. It does not mean that we allow unrighteousness to exist in our midst. To be forgiving and loving does not at all mean being weak.[7]

As of this writing, the political parties in the U.S. have become such opposing forces that hardly any work for the common good can get done. An exceptionally unusual election has left a component of our society bitter and angry. Protests against actions of the newly elected president are taking place across the nation. There are cries of racial injustice all around the country. The wealth gap between the poor and the rich is the largest it's ever been. In the world around us, there is continual battling in Jerusalem with Jews and Muslims killing each other over land rights. There are wars and violence in Iraq, Syria, and Afghanistan. There are vicious, murdering "clans" like Boko Haram, ISIS, and others, who feel they have a right to kidnap, enslave, and rape children and to massacre innocent "non-believers" in the name of their religions. Our country is invested in some way in dealing with all of this.

Changing the entrenched mindsets that create perpetual problems and wars like these will take something quite extraordinary—something greater and more different than anything we've ever tried. The extraordinary forgiveness that God has shared with us, the forgiveness that is truly driven by tenacious love and is willing to die for that cause, is the only power strong enough to change the way of the world. It is the only way we will finally be able to beat our "swords into plowshares."[8] The people of the world, including world leaders, have a lot of growing up to do. And as ambassadors of Christ, we are the ones commissioned to help them.

Can't you see how the kingdom of God will build up if we share the good news through a forgiving and loving presence, so that others will learn to believe and do the same? Can't you see the people released from prison being helped to build new lives away from the troubled communities where they learned the wrong way to live? Can't you see the disciples of God taking the lead to change how we see victims of sexual violence and sex trafficking, and finding ways to give people we call "prostitutes" a new lease on life? Can't you see believers working to build bridges between people of different races, cultures, economic status, and mindsets to replace the walls between them that breed division, hate, and strife?

Can't you imagine the whole world becoming safer and more productive because we have not only found ways to share the wealth but have also found ways to bring peace through forgiveness and love? Can't you rejoice in the idea that one day we might decrease our investments in manufacturing weapons of death and destruction and increase our investments in helping and healing others? That's the kingdom of God come to earth as it is in heaven. These are the "greater things" disciples of Christ are to help make happen here and now. This is what the new world created through a revolutionized Christianity looks like, and it can only happen when humans mature enough to learn how to live simply, to truly love, and to truly forgive. It is difficult work, work to which we are to give priority over meeting our own routine maintenance. But it's the only kind of work that truly makes life worthwhile.

Deepen

This is an excerpt from a *New York Times* article on the massacre at Emanuel A.M.E. Church in Charleston, North Carolina, on June 17, 2015:

> The mass murder of nine people who gathered Wednesday night for Bible study at a landmark black church has shaken a city whose history from slavery to the Civil War to the present is inseparable from the nation's anguished struggle with race.
>
> Fourteen hours after the massacre at Emanuel African Methodist Episcopal Church, in which the Rev. Clementa

C. Pinckney, the church pastor and a prominent state sena-
tor, was among the dead, the police in Shelby, N.C., acting
on a tip from a motorist, on Thursday arrested Dylann
Storm Roof, a 21-year-old white man with an unsettled
personal life and a recent history of anti-black views.

The killings, with victims ranging in age from 26 to 87,
left people stunned and grieving. Witnesses said Mr. Roof
sat with church members for an hour and then started
venting against African-Americans and opened fire on the
group.

At a bond hearing for Dylann Roof two days later,
several members of the church, family members of the
victims, speaking directly to Roof, told him that they
"prayed for his soul" and that they forgave him.[9]

Next is a National Public Radio story dated October 2,
2007, titled "Amish Forgive School Shooter, Struggle with
Grief." It aired on "All Things Considered" one year after
the October 2, 2006, shooting at a one-room Amish schoolhouse in Nickel Mines, Pennsylvania, when Charles Carl
Roberts IV took hostages and shot ten girls (aged 6 to 13),
killing five, before committing suicide in the schoolhouse:

It's been a week for quiet reflection in the Amish communities around Nickel Mines, PA, which one year ago
experienced tragedy.

It was in the tiny community that a man stormed into
a one-room schoolhouse and shot 10 young girls, killing
five. He then killed himself. That old school has since
been demolished. The new school was closed on the one-
year anniversary and families met privately in prayer.

Since the tragedy, people around the world have been in-
spired by the way the Amish expressed forgiveness toward
the killer and his family. But while their acts of forgiveness
were inspiring, they also caused a misperception that the
Amish had quickly gotten over the tragedy. . . .

Charles Roberts wasn't Amish, but Amish families knew
him as the milk truck driver who made deliveries. Last

month, it was announced that the Amish community had donated money to the killer's widow and her three young children.

It was one more gesture of forgiveness, gestures that began soon after the shooting.[10]

The willingness of these two groups of Christians to forgive so quickly after losing their loved ones in such tragic ways astounded the public and caused a great deal of discussion about why anyone would do such a thing. Critics of their willingness to forgive include those who just didn't understand it, those who believed it to be unnatural, and those who suggested it took away the necessity to grieve in a proper way. For example, Dawn Turner, a reporter for the *Chicago Tribune*, reflected on the Emanuel Church shooting from an African American perspective:

> I have to admit that although I am humbled by Emanuel's stories of forgiveness, I'm equally conflicted. As a Christian, I understand that forgiveness is the cornerstone of the faith. But I also know that religion long has been used to force compliance in followers and tamp down impulses that feel natural and necessary.[11]

Some commentators criticized the quick and complete forgiveness with which the Amish responded, arguing that forgiveness is inappropriate when no remorse has been expressed, and that such an attitude runs the risk of denying the existence of evil."[12]

INDIVIDUAL DEEPENING EXERCISES

1. Take some time to think about how the combination of a welcoming, loving, and nonjudgmental environment, like the one found at Shades of Grace church, helps to bring healing to people who are struggling with drug or alcohol addictions, who are homeless, or who might suffer with mental difficulties. How have you experienced (or failed to experience) such an environment in your faith community?

2. Meditate on how difficult it must have been for the people in both of the situations described in the Deepen section to forgive the persons who killed their loved ones. Imagine the pain and loss of having a child, parent, husband, or wife killed in such a senseless and unexpected way. Place yourselves at the feet of the cross, where Jesus hung and said, "Father, forgive them; for they know not what they do." Allow his forgiveness to help you to understand the depth of love that he has for us, and to understand that this is the kind of love he wants us to share with others, even mentally ill people who kill children. Pray for the families who have suffered but who were still willing to forgive because they are believers in Christ, who died forgiving them.

3. Take some time to meditate on whether you need to truly forgive someone for hurting or harming you. Read Luke 23:20-35. Place yourself on the cross, with the person who hurt you at the foot of the cross, mocking and taunting you. Imagine that you have the power to either destroy that person or to forgive them. Pray to be able to forgive that person as Jesus has forgiven you. The ability to forgive may not come at once; it may take a while. But continue to work on it in your prayers and meditation times as long as necessary, with the hope that you will be able to think of that person and the situation without any anger, and with true forgiveness and the desire to love them in your heart. If you cannot imagine ever coming to that place of forgiveness, take the time to acknowledge the grief, the rage, the trauma, or other emotions that make forgiveness unthinkable. How are you dealing with those emotions, if at all? How might your faith equip you to cope and press through such pain?

GROUP DISCUSSION

1. Review the chapter.

(a) Do you agree with the author's statement: "Learning to freely forgive others is another crucial component of effectively praying the Lord's Prayer because our willingness to forgive proves to the world that the greatest power of all is God's love"? Why or why not?

(b) How does Jesus' death on the cross prove the author's statement: "We cannot truly love others if we are unable to truly forgive them"?

(c) What does the author mean: "We cannot be the salt and light in the world that we must be in order to build God's kingdom on earth if we do not learn to truly forgive others"?

(d) Ask the group to discuss their experiences with being forgiven and how it makes them feel.

2. Discuss some of your thoughts relating to Individual Deepening Exercise #1.

3. Read aloud the Deepen section of this chapter. Share how you felt when you learned about the brutality committed against these two very different faith communities. Sadness and anger are natural reactions to injustice and evil. Discuss whether it is possible to truly forgive someone while you are still grieving over what they did to you. Can you force true forgiveness when you are feeling outraged by someone's actions? Do you agree that the immediate willingness to forgive "runs the risk of denying the existence of evil"? Why do you think we find so many ways of denying the virtue of being willing to freely forgive others?

4. In Matthew 18:21-22, Peter asks Jesus whether he should forgive a person who sins against him up to seven times. Jesus responds by telling Peter he should forgive seventy-seven times, which can also be interpreted as seventy multiplied by seven times, meaning an infinite number of times.[13] Jesus wants him, and us, to understand that we should not be counting the number of times we forgive someone—we are simply to forgive. Discuss whether you believe it is humanly possible for someone to truly forgive the same person over and over again. How might this text be used to lead to continuing abusive behavior? Discuss the important balance between understanding how to forgive and taking steps to prevent abusive behavior.

5. Discuss this quote from a 1957 sermon by Rev. Dr. Martin Luther King Jr., entitled "Loving Your Enemies": "[One] who is devoid of the power to forgive is devoid of the power to love. It is impossible even to begin the act of loving one's enemies without the prior acceptance of the necessity, over and over again, of forgiving those who inflict evil and injury upon us."[14] Discuss how Dr. King's nonviolent approach to protesting legalized segregation in the United States reflected his Christian faith. Share what you know about U.S. law and culture changes that resulted because of the Civil Rights Movement he led. Discuss what social inequities still need to be addressed. Will Dr. King's methods still work in today's world? Why or why not?

NOTES

1. "Shades of Grace: New Church with Curious Name Discovers Forgotten Community," The Call, Annette Spence, Editor, vol. E15, Number 10, updated May 25, 2015. The opening story is taken, with permission, from this article. Read more: http://holston.org/about/communications/the-call/volE15/num10/.

2. Martin Luther King Jr., *Strength to Love* (New York: Harper & Row, 1963), 34. According to the website mlkonline.net, this sermon was delivered at Dexter Avenue Baptist Church on November 17, 1957.

3. See, e.g., John 15:18-19: "If the world hates you, be aware that it hated me before it hated you. If you belonged to the world, the world would love you as its own. Because you do not belong to the world, but I have chosen you out of the world—therefore the world hates you."

4. James Mulholland also makes the connection between loving others and being forgiven by God: "Until we eliminate poverty, everything else we do is a mockery of God's will. . . . We cannot pray, 'Forgive us our sins,' with sincerity if we continue to allow children to starve to death. There is no sin greater than allowing some of our brothers or sisters to die when we have the capacity to save them." James Mulholland, *Praying Like Jesus: The Lord's Prayer in a Culture of Prosperity* (San Francisco: HarperCollins, 2001), 87.

5. See N. T. Wright, *The Lord and His Prayer* (Grand Rapids: William B. Eerdmans Publishing Company, 1996), 57: "The church is to be the advance guard of the great act of Forgiveness of Sins that God intends to accomplish for the entire cosmos. Justice and peace, truth and mercy, will one day reign in God's world; and the church, who could almost be defined as the people who pray the Lord's Prayer, is to model and pioneer the way of life which is, actually, the *only* way of life, because it is the way of forgiveness."

6. "He Looked Beyond My Fault and Saw My Need," lyrics composed by Dottie Rambo, 2003.

> Amazing grace shall always be my song of praise.
> For it was grace, that brought me liberty,
> I'll never know, just why Christ came to love me so.
> He looked beyond my faults and saw my need.
>
> I shall forever lift mine eyes to Calvary,
> To view the cross, where Jesus died for me.
> How marvelous, his grace that caught my falling soul,
> He looked beyond all my faults and saw my need. . . .

7. William H. Willimon and Stanley Hauerwas put it this way: "In commanding us to forgive others Jesus is not saying that the injustice we have suffered is inconsequential. . . . Rather, Jesus is refusing to let sin have the last word in our story. In commanding us to forgive, Jesus is not producing a race of doormats, a new set of victims who, having been slapped on the right cheek, offer the left as well so that they may be twice victimized. Jesus has no interest in producing victims; the world produces enough. Rather in com-

manding us to forgive, Jesus is inviting us to take charge, to turn the world around, to throw a monkey wrench in the eternal wheel of retribution and vengeance. . . . We can take charge, turn things around, be victors rather than victims. We can forgive." William H. Willimon and Stanley Hauerwas, *Lord, Teach Us: The Lord's Prayer & the Christian Life* (Nashville: Abingdon Press, 1996), 84.

8. Isaiah 2:1-4: "The word that Isaiah son of Amoz saw concerning Judah and Jerusalem. In days to come the mountain of the Lord's house shall be established as the highest of the mountains, and shall be raised above the hills; all the nations shall stream to it. Many peoples shall come and say, 'Come, let us go up to the mountain of the Lord, to the house of the God of Jacob; that he may teach us his ways and that we may walk in his paths.' For out of Zion shall go forth instruction, and the word of the Lord from Jerusalem. He shall judge between the nations, and shall arbitrate for many peoples; they shall beat their swords into plowshares, and their spears into pruning hooks; nation shall not lift up sword against nation, neither shall they learn war any more."

9. Read more: http://www.nytimes.com/2015/06/19/us/charleston-church-shooting.html.

10. Read more: http://www.npr.org/templates/story/story.php?storyId=14900930.

11. Read more: http://www.chicagotribune.com/news/columnists/ct-emanuel-church-charleston-dawn-turner-20150928-column.html.

12. Read more: http://cross-currents.com/2006/10/17/not-always-divine/ See also Jacoby, Jeff (October 8, 2006). "Undeserved forgiveness," *The Boston Globe*.

13. "The Greek number can be legitimately understood as 'seventy-seven times'. . . or 'four hundred ninety times.' . . . The difference between Peter's proposal and Jesus' pronouncement is not a matter of math or linguistics, but of the nature of forgiveness. Whoever counts has not forgiven at all, but is only biding his or her time. The kind of forgiveness called for is beyond all calculation. . . ." M. Eugene Boring, "The Gospel of Matthew," *The New Interpreter's Bible,* vol. VIII, ed. Leander E. Keck, et. al. (Nashville: Abingdon Press, 1995), 380.

14. King, *Strength to Love*, 35.

Chapter 7
"And lead us not into temptation"

The disciples asked Jesus to teach them to pray out of a desire to be the best disciples they could be, and that they would understand that the petition to not be led into temptation related to being effective disciples. Just as Jesus was tempted in the wilderness to take the "easy" route by Satan, one temptation that we as disciples face is to rest comfortably instead of being the world-changers we are called to be. The problem we face is that the temptation to stay comfortable doesn't feel like temptation at all. Our story for this chapter helps us to see how we may be called to go to places we never thought we'd go and to do things we never thought we'd do when we allow our hearts to break over the harm people do to others who are vulnerable. It helps us to understand that we must not allow our comfort to tempt us away from the often difficult mission work we are called to as Christ's disciples.

Life in Our Time

Claudia Hamm was an active member of the Presbyterian Women, an independent organization within the Presbyterian Church (USA) of more than 300,000 women. The Presbyterian Women made human trafficking one of their top mission priorities in 2012. In an article from the Presbyterian Church's magazine *Presbyterians Today*, we're told that this priority is what made Hamm, who was the moderator of Presbyterian Women of San Jose Presbytery, begin to pay attention to the news about human trafficking. "I'm a grandmother of a 16-year-old girl," Hamm is reported as saying. "There's a market for girls like her—even younger than her. It's a hard thing to come to grips with."

When she found out that the Super Bowl was coming to Santa Clara in 2016, and that the Super Bowl is also known to be a place where trafficking occurs, she and the other women were shocked and felt the need to do something. So they went to work. They held a human trafficking forum in March 2015. They discovered that California is believed to be one of the nation's top destinations for traffickers. They later connected with some 50 agencies and 1,500 activists at a Bay Area Anti-Trafficking Coalition event, including Freedom House, a nonprofit organization that works with law enforcement and community partners to identify survivors of trafficking and to help them rebuild their lives.

Hamm now volunteers at one of the Freedom House homes. "Some of these girls are younger than my granddaughter," she says. "Many are from foster homes, as young as 11 and 12. It's so dark, what humans will do for money."

"It's pure evil," says Freedom House founder Jaida Im. "These children are the runaways, the throwaways. It's just abuse, after abuse, after abuse."

Hamm helps to train personnel in the hotel and motel industry so that they can better recognize trafficking, and stays in communication with the agencies involved in the Bay Area Anti-Trafficking Coalition.[1]

"And lead us not into temptation"

James 1:13-14 tells us: "No one, when tempted, should say, 'I am being tempted by God'; for God cannot be tempted by evil and he himself tempts no one. But one is tempted by one's own desire, being lured and enticed by it. . . ." This helps us to understand that this petition is not about God leading us to do wrong; it has to do with helping us deal with the temptations that we will most certainly face. Many scholars see this phrase of the prayer as a request to God not to test us more than we can handle.[2] Jesus wants his disciples to pray that God will both protect and guide us in times of trial as well as strengthen us so that we will not be lured or "dragged away" (NIV) by our own desires.[3]

From a disciple's perspective, this petition must be understood as a request to not let us stray from the high calling that God has created for us. Jesus surely knows how difficult the struggle to do God's will can be in the midst of the many temptations we face in this world. Our spirits may be willing, but our flesh is weak. We need always to pray for God's help and support to keep us from straying.

Jesus wants his disciples to stay focused on the primary work—going out to share the good news with the world through our words, teachings, and actions. This is the work that must be done in order for God's kingdom to come to earth, and it is to be our first love, our highest goal, our most important job to do here and now. We must constantly guard against temptations that lead us away from this priority, and they are abundant.

The temptations we face as disciples are not limited to what we normally think of as evil or sin. We can be pulled away from God's work by things that do not seem wrong to us at all. What feels like normal behavior can be yielding to temptation when it prevents us from doing the work we're called to do as Christians. Because these behaviors seem normal, they become "veiled," or hidden from us, so that we do not see them as temptations. These veiled temptations can be more disastrous to the work of building God's kingdom on earth than things we clearly label as sin and evil, because they can gradually draw us away from our first priority without our realizing it.

I believe this may be what happened to the church in Ephesus, as revealed in Revelation 2:1-7, where Jesus lauded the Ephesians for their hard work, their perseverance, their intolerance for wickedness, and their endurance. Yet, he said to them, "But I have this against you, that you have abandoned the love you had at first. Remember then from what you have fallen; repent, and do the works you did at first." I believe the "works [they] did at first" would include what Jesus taught his disciples to do when he was here on earth: to boldly share the gospel in the world, going out to both show and tell the world, "The kingdom of God has come near to you" (Luke 10:9).

Had the gathered community begun to focus too much on themselves, and not enough on the world around them? The Ephesians were doing well in many ways, and Jesus commended them for that work, but what they did well—toil, patience, endurance, righteousness, discernment, and strength—all may have been inwardly focused. Their good work did not seem to include going out to "every town and place where [Jesus] himself intended to go," as he told his disciples to do in Luke 10.[4] If they were not sharing the news of Christ through their words and deeds with the world around them, then they were drifting away from the most important thing they were to do. They had been tempted away from what should have been their first love without recognizing what happened.

We are all subject to falling away from the most important work that we are to do for Christ, often in ways that may be difficult for us to see. We don't see them because they have become normal behavior; they are veiled from us by normality. One veiled temptation that we face today is similar to what happened to the church in Ephesus. Just like that church, many of today's churches have become inwardly focused. This happens so easily when there is so much to do to plan the worship services, maintain the building, care for the sick, encourage the bonding of church members, and so on. Keeping the church operating and caring for the members can keep pastors and churches quite busy, and can easily turn our priorities inward rather than looking outward to the needs of the community and the world that Jesus wants to reach.

There are many other hidden temptations in modern churches as well, such as giving undue priority to individual comfort, which happens when believers are taught that God wants them to prosper but they are not taught about the commitments that God wants back from them or the limits and dangers of earthly prosperity. Another veiled temptation is expecting the church to "fit in" with society, instead of the other way around. This happens when disciples wrap the American flag around the church, making our faith an extension of patriotism instead of offering to our nation the prophetic voice of God that speaks God's truth, justice, and righteousness to those in power. Another is prioritizing personal faith and piety over community and kingdom building to such an extent that the church has "faith without works."[5]

Other veiled temptations include:

- Prioritizing activities and events among church members above sharing God's love with the surrounding community (the "social club" church).

- Using our family obligations as excuses to limit the time we spend working for God, rather than helping our families prioritize faith and join in the work.[6]

- Thinking that the way we exercise our faith is in competition with other Christian groups and good people of other faith traditions, such that we are not willing to work together with them to accomplish the common goal of kingdom building.

- Focusing our energy on divisive judgmental issues on which Christians often disagree, such as abortion and homosexuality, rather than on sharing the unfathomable love and healing presence of Christ with those who need to feel and understand it.

There are many other ways we can slip away from our kingdom-building work without recognizing what we've done. These temptations decrease the strength and effectiveness of discipleship and take away our power to bring the kingdom of God to earth, making us unable to be the salt of the earth or the shining lights that are needed so desperately in this world. As we saw in Chapter 4, here in the United States, which many call a Christian society, both poverty and imprisonment are higher than in many other countries. Have U.S. churches failed to do their part to help make our society a place where, in the words of the prophet Amos, ". . .justice rolls down like waters, and righteousness like an ever-flowing stream" (Amos 5:24)?

Jesus Set the Example

We have two potent examples of Jesus dealing with temptation. The first occurs right after his baptism at the beginning of his ministry, when he was led by the Spirit into the wilderness to be tempted by the devil for forty days (see Luke 4:1-12). The other is when Jesus goes to the Mount of Olives near the end of his ministry, right before he was about to be arrested, tried, beaten, and sentenced to die by crucifixion (see Luke 22:39-44).

In the wilderness, Jesus was tempted to use his powers to help himself by turning stone into bread after fasting for forty days, he was offered authority over all the world if he would only worship the devil, and he was tempted to test God by throwing himself off the high pinnacle of the temple. We know he did not succumb to any of these temptations, which all were designed to test his willingness to take an easier way than God had planned for him.

The temptation on the Mount of Olives was more difficult for him. He admitted to God that his spirit was willing, but that his flesh was weak. He asked God to take away the "cup" of pain and sorrow that he knew he was about to experience, and he was so distressed that his sweat turned to blood. But he found the strength to say, "Yet not my will, but yours be done," and went on to offer himself to the authorities.

Jesus knows how easy it is for us to fall away, to fall asleep when there is difficult work to be done. The flesh truly is weak. So he wants us to pray that God will help us to not be led away from our discipleship work, lest we become unable to stand against the continued and unrelenting injustice and unrighteousness that has taken root in our world.

His great temptations make ours seem small, but they let us know that he understands what it's like to be human. Knowing that Jesus understands what we go through should both comfort us and strengthen our willpower.

Living Like We Mean It

If we want to live like we don't want to be tempted, then of course, we must deal with all kinds of obvious temptations—the ones that are included on those lists of sinful things in the Bible, such as sexual immorality, impurity, idolatry, hatred, discord, jealousy, rage, selfish ambition, dissensions, envy, drunkenness, orgies, and the like (see Galatians 5:19-21, NIV). It is right and good to avoid such obvious transgressions, a basic step for those who come to believe in Christ.

As we grow deeper in faith, however, we must also constantly measure our actions against the true call to be disciples of Christ. We must constantly reflect on what we actually do as people of faith. If all of our faith efforts are directed toward things like building our personal faith, taking care of the church building, or socializing with other church members, then we may have already been led away from what ought to be our first love as followers of Christ. When we fashion our Christian walks to fit neatly and safely into our social setting, limit our faith to fit comfortably around other family and work obligations, or if we waste our limited time on condemning and judging those who don't agree with us, we simply will not become the world-changers that God needs us to be.

We must grow beyond the belief level of new Christians into the mature faith of disciples who understand that more is demanded of us than just being good people. There are lots of good people in this world who are not Christians. We are called to grow beyond personal piety to become the world-changers that Christ intends us to be. And more is demanded of us than trying to make everyone agree with our views on divisive issues. There are lots of good Christians in this world who hold different views about what it means to be faithful. When we allow our differences to divide us, our power to make a difference is greatly weakened.

To become the salt of the earth and the light for the world that Jesus intends us to be, we must go out into the world as commissioned disciples, bringing the good news to those who need to both hear and feel it. We must resist the temptation to believe we can accomplish God's will by taking the easy paths in life. Each of us must pray to God to help us avoid the very difficult temptations that would keep us in our own comfortable places, where we offer only minimal efforts to help others. Like Claudia Hamm, Jeanne Alert, and Rev. Will Shewey, we must learn about the grim realities that other people face in life and, using our gifts of time, intelligence, and strength, we must work with others to serve them in ways that will help them feel and understand the love of God.

The way to know a kingdom-building project is to envision the outcome of the work. Will what you are doing bring good news to someone by making their life better? Will the demons of hunger, poverty, racism, sexism, sexual exploitation, intolerance—you name them—be driven out in Jesus' name through the work that you do? If so, then that is the kingdom-building work you are called to do.

If we go out to share the good news of the kingdom as Jesus directed his disciples, we'll be able to come back, rejoicing that "in your name even the demons submit to us!"[7] We'll feel the power of Jesus' joy, rejoicing with us through the Holy Spirit over what we've been able to accomplish. What great joy! This is joy that the world can never take away from us.

Deepen

We conclude this chapter with deepening material that once again focuses on labor and sex trafficking. I guess by now you know that this is an important issue to me. I cannot imagine a terror worse than the forced and often violent sexual abuse of a child, committed multiple times, night after night, in order to make some depraved person wealthy. Human trafficking is highlighted in this book because standing against it is one thing that I believe most Christians can agree on. In spite of all of the differences among the Christian body of believers, I believe we can agree that trafficking of humans, and especially children, is an evil that must be stopped. And, as shown in Chapter 1 in the Joint Declaration of Religious Leaders Against Modern Slavery, it is an issue that major religions can also come together over. Dealing with the scourge of human trafficking in our world is a good place to start the Christian revolution!

Each year, the U.S. Department of State publishes a Trafficking in Persons Report. Included in these reports are short stories about victims of human trafficking. What follows are some of the stories published in the 2016 report.

VIETNAM | CHINA: When Ping was 12 years old, an acquaintance offered her and a friend jobs in a different city in Vietnam. Ping and her friend accepted the offer. The recruiter took them to a local bus station and placed them on a bus with their "caretaker." When they disembarked, the caretaker revealed they were in China and had been sold into prostitution with 20 other girls. When one of the girls refused to do as she was told, the owners beat her severely. Ping suffered in the brothel for almost a year before authorities raided the establishment, rescued the girls, and returned them to Vietnam. Although Ping still suffers from headaches and poor vision—including moments of blindness—as a result of her exploitation, she is training for a career in hairdressing.

HUNGARY | UNITED STATES: Michael was looking for jobs on the internet when he met Lorant, who offered him the chance to earn a lot of money working as a male escort in the United States. Michael and several other men accepted the offer, left Hungary, and traveled to Florida, where Lorant instead forced them into prostitution for 18–20 hours each day without pay. Lorant forced eight men to stay in a one-bedroom apartment, confiscated their identity documents, and threatened to kill them if they asked to leave. Police discovered the trafficking scheme after neighbors reported unusual behavior outside the men's living quarters. Lorant was convicted of human trafficking and racketeering and sentenced to 11 years in prison.

NIGERIA | UNITED KINGDOM: When a British-Nigerian couple offered to take Paul, 14 years old, from Nigeria to the UK, enroll him in school, and pay him to perform housework, he accepted. Once in Britain, however, the family changed his name and added him to their family passport as an adopted son. They forced him to clean their house for as many as 17 hours each day for no pay and did not allow him to go to school. They took his passport, set up cameras to monitor his movements, and limited his contact with the outside world. Paul tried several times to escape; once he contacted the police, who told him they did not handle family matters. Eight years after that, Paul heard a radio report about modern slavery and bravely reached out to an NGO. The NGO helped, and the couple was arrested a few months later after having exploited Paul for 24 years. They each received 10-year sentences, six years for servitude and four for other crimes.

SYRIA | LEBANON: Recruiters came to Angela's town in Syria offering paid work in restaurants or hotels in Lebanon, and Angela accepted the opportunity to leave her war-torn country. Once in Lebanon, she was subjected to sex trafficking along with more than 70 other women and girls, many of whom were also Syrian. The traffickers locked the girls in hotels and barred their windows. They subjected the women to sex trafficking for more than two months, sometimes forcing them to see 20 clients each day. The traffickers also raped and tortured the girls into submission. One day Angela and three others took advantage of a momentary lapse in security and escaped. They boarded a bus and confided in the driver. He reported the incident to the police, who raided the premises, helped release the other victims, and arrested 18 suspected traffickers. Authorities referred 35 of the victims to a women's shelter for assistance, while the others chose to return home.

UNITED STATES: Nina ran away from home at age 14. She met a woman who put her up in a hotel room and brought her "clients." For the next 13 years, Nina had 20 different pimps who advertised her for sex on the internet and abused her verbally and physically. By the time she was finally referred to victim services, Nina had been convicted of 52 offenses, mostly prostitution—her first conviction at age 16—and spent time in both juvenile hall and jail.

CANADA: Holly, 13 years old, didn't recognize Emilie on Facebook, but seeing they had mutual friends, accepted her friend request. Holly and Emilie chatted and quickly became online friends. One day Emilie told Holly that her boyfriend had found them both jobs that would make them a lot of money. Emilie asked Holly to come to her apartment that weekend. When Holly arrived, Emilie, her boyfriend, and another man told Holly she had to have sex with men for money. When Holly refused, they threatened to hurt her. They posted photos of Holly on an escort website and took her to different cities around Canada to have sex with paying clients. One day, when Emilie's boyfriend left the room, Holly fled and received help from a passerby. All three perpetrators have been charged with numerous crimes, including sex trafficking, and await trial.[8]

INDIVIDUAL DEEPENING EXERCISES

1. Read Revelation 2:1-7. Imagine God speaking to you and evaluating your Christian walk in a similar way. What would God applaud you for doing well? What do you think God would hold against you? If there is some way you feel you are falling short, pray to God to give you the strength and wisdom to do better. Then sit down and write out a plan that will help you do it.

2. Take a few minutes to remember what you were like when you were a young teenager, between twelve and fifteen years old. Try to imagine what it would have felt like at that age to have been tricked, coerced, or forcefully taken to be sold over and over again to be sexually abused by sick adults so that your slaver could become rich. Imagine the slavers taking you away from your family and home, keeping you in place with beatings or drugs and threatening to kill members of your family if you went to the police. What do you think happens to the minds of young children who are enslaved this way for years and years? What would you want someone to do for you if you were being trafficked? What can you do to help children who have become trapped in sex trafficking?

3. Think about some ways you can help share the good news through kingdom building in your local community by working to help bring healing and hope to problems such as poverty, gangs, trafficking, and so on. Do some research on what community organizations are involved in fighting against something that draws your attention, then go to the site and talk to people there to determine if there is a role for your help.

GROUP DISCUSSION

1. Review the chapter.

(a) According to the author, what should be the "first love" of mature disciples?

(b) What does the author mean by "veiled temptations"? Take a few minutes to review some of the temptations mentioned.

(c) Discuss what you believe the author means: "As we grow deeper in faith, however, we must also constantly measure our actions against the true call to be disciples of Christ."

2. Discuss whether your own church or group may need to face some "veiled temptations," either those mentioned in this lesson or others. Include in your discussion some ways to address the problems you discuss.

3. How does the work of Claudia Hamm and the Presbyterian Women exemplify sharing the good news about the coming of God's kingdom? Why did they do it? What obstacles do you think they may have had to overcome, as people of faith, in order to become engaged in this work? Discuss whether you think your faith group or church would want to become involved in the battle against human trafficking, either locally, nationally, or internationally.[9]

4. Go back to Chapter 1 and review together the Joint Declaration of Religious Leaders Against Modern Slavery. Discuss the international components of human trafficking that these leaders are challenging, evidenced by the excerpts from the State Department's Trafficking in Persons Report. Do you think the cooperation among religious leaders will be a big step forward in combatting such a global problem? Why or why not? How can a local church like yours be involved?

NOTES

1. Paul Seebeck, "Human trafficking: beyond the Super Bowl," *Presbyterians Today*: February 1, 2016. Read more: http://www .pcusa.org/news/2016/2/1/human-trafficking-beyond-super-bowl/.

2. See N. T. Wright, *The Lord and His Prayer* (Grand Rapids: William B. Eerdmans Publishing Company, 1996), 73: "To say 'lead us not into temptation' does not, of course, mean that God himself causes people to be tempted. It has, rather, three levels of meaning. First, it means 'let us escape the great tribulation, the great testing, that is coming on all the world.'. . . . it means 'do not let us be led into temptation that we will be unable to bear'. . . and . . . it means 'enable us to pass safely through the testing of our faith.'"

3. See R. Alan Culpepper, "The Gospel of Luke," *The New Interpreter's Bible,* vol. IX, ed. Leander E. Keck, et. al. (Nashville: Abingdon Press, 1995), 235: ". . . [T]he model prayer appeals to God as the One who controls all of life for deliverance from any trials that will threaten either our confession of the 'thy' petitions . . . or God's provision of our physical and spiritual needs (the 'our' petitions)."

4. See the discussions about the disciples being sent out in Chapters 1 and 4.

5. See James 2:26: "For just as the body without the spirit is dead, so faith without works is also dead."

6. See Luke 9:57-62: "As they were going along the road, someone said to him, 'I will follow you wherever you go.' And Jesus said
to him, 'Foxes have holes, and birds of the air have nests; but the
Son of Man has nowhere to lay his head.' To another he said, 'Follow me.' But he said, 'Lord, first let me go and bury my father.' But
Jesus said to him, 'Let the dead bury their own dead; but as for you,
go and proclaim the kingdom of God.' Another said, 'I will follow
you, Lord; but let me first say farewell to those at my home.' Jesus
said to him, 'No one who puts a hand to the plow and looks back
is fit for the kingdom of God.'"

7. Luke 10:17-23: "The seventy returned with joy, saying, 'Lord,
in your name even the demons submit to us!' He said to them, 'I
watched Satan fall from heaven like a flash of lightning. See, I have
given you authority to tread on snakes and scorpions, and over all
the power of the enemy; and nothing will hurt you. Nevertheless,
do not rejoice at this, that the spirits submit to you, but rejoice that
your names are written in heaven.'"

8. Read more: http://www.state.gov/j/tip/rls/tiprpt/2016/258687
.htm. "The victims' testimonies included in this Report are meant
to be illustrative and to characterize the many forms of trafficking and the wide variety of places in which they occur. They do
not reflect all forms of human trafficking and could take place
almost anywhere in the world. Many of the victims' names have
been changed in this Report. Most photographs are not images of
confirmed trafficking victims. They illustrate the myriad forms of
exploitation that comprise human trafficking and the variety of situations in which trafficking victims are found." U.S. State Department Trafficking in Persons Report, 2016.

9. If you'd like more information about how to become involved in combating human trafficking, here are some informative
websites: http://polarisproject.org, http://sharedhope.org, http://
traffickingresourcecenter.org.

Chapter 8
Empowering the Prayer

Now that we've examined the prayer that Jesus taught his disciples carefully, we're concluding by looking more deeply at Christianity in the world today, some difficulties we face, and some things that give us hope. Our story for this chapter is about an entrenched problem that America has not yet been able to come to grips with: the ongoing struggle of racial discrimination and discord. Achieving racial justice and reconciliation is one societal problem that I believe can only be resolved with the loving guidance of Christian leadership because it involves both the confession of sin, or admitting wrongdoing, and a sincere willingness to forgive. This is the kind of work I believe the Lord's Prayer is intended to empower us to accomplish.

Life in Our Time

On July 12, 2016, a memorial service was held in Dallas to honor five police officers killed in a shooting during a Black Lives Matter demonstration. President Obama gave a speech there that "sought to unify a nation left divided and raw."[1] The demonstration five days prior had stemmed from the July 5 fatal shooting by Baton Rouge police of Alton Sterling while he was pinned to the ground, and the July 6 fatal shooting by police in Minnesota of Philando Castile while he was in his car with his fiancée. The following news story reflects how the toxic combination of gun proliferation, gun violence, racial animosity, and social injustice have come together at the time of this writing to cause great chaos in our country.

The Washington Post

In Dallas, Obama seeks to soothe tensions between civilians and police

By Louisa Loveluck, William Wan and Mark Berman
July 12, 2016

DALLAS—President Obama sought to unify a nation left divided and raw by recent fatal shootings involving police officers, speaking Tuesday at a memorial service for five officers killed here and calling for understanding from both law enforcement and those protesting against them. In his latest visit to a city heartbroken by a mass shooting, Obama tried to ease the tensions that have erupted in recent days—first when black men in Louisiana and Minnesota were fatally shot by police, then when a gunman who said he was angry over police killings opened fire on officers in Dallas. Obama praised police officers and sharply criticized those who would paint all police as bigoted or seek violence against law enforcement, yet he also acknowledged the very real fear and pain among black Americans who have felt targeted or mistreated by officers. . . .

Even as he spoke of unity, there were still tangible signs of a rift between protesters and police. Obama was interrupted by applause when he spoke in a concert hall filled with law enforcement officials about those officers killed last Thursday, but the families of those officers did not clap when he spoke about the "Black Lives Matter" protests or invoked the killings in Minnesota and Louisiana.

"Your work, the work of police officers across the country, is like no other," Obama said. "From the moment you put on that uniform, you have answered a call that at any moment, even in the briefest interaction, may put your life in harm's way."

Consoling a nation after a violent episode has become familiar ground for Obama, whose presidency has been marked by tragedies and attacks in places such as a school in Newtown, Conn.; a church in Charleston, S.C.; an office holiday party in San Bernardino, Calif.; and many others.

"I'm not naivë," Obama said. "I've spoken at too many memorials during the course of this presidency. I've hugged too many families that lost a loved one to senseless violence."

In Dallas, the attack on police during a peaceful protest against police shootings marked a sudden, violent intersection of two issues that have dominated the country during Obama's presidency: Outrage over how police use force, particularly deadly force, and the unending string of mass shootings that have brought Obama to cities such as San Bernardino; Roseburg, Ore.; Charleston; and, most recently, Orlando. Obama's remarks Tuesday—addressing the single deadliest day for law enforcement since the Sept. 11, 2001 terrorist attacks—came on the one-month anniversary of the shooting rampage in an Orlando nightclub, the worst mass shooting in U.S. history. Over the weekend, Obama said that even in the face of the mass shooting in Dallas and the still-roiling protests elsewhere, he believed the country was not irreparably fractured.

"As painful as this week has been, I firmly believe that America is not as divided as some have suggested," he said during a NATO summit in Warsaw.

In recent days, demonstrations have broken out from New York to San Francisco after deaths of black men in Minnesota and Louisiana, evoking the protests that erupted after deaths in Ferguson, Mo., and Baltimore in recent years. Protesters in Atlanta staged a sit-in in front of the governor's mansion late Monday. In Baton Rouge—one of the main flash points—the American Civil Liberties Union of Louisiana complained Monday of police using "violent, militarized tactics" that have included more than 200 arrests in recent days.[2]

The Power of Heartfelt Prayer

First Samuel 1 tells us that a woman named Hannah, beloved wife of Elkanah, wanted a male child more than anything in the world. She prayed and prayed, but her prayers were not answered until the day she arose from her depressed state to go to the Temple to pray again. That day she prayed so deeply that Eli, the priest, thought she was drunk. In that prayer she made a promise to God that matched what God had wanted from her all along: she promised that her child would be given back to the Lord to be dedicated to the priesthood. Hannah had no way of knowing what God needed, but her promise was what God had been waiting for. When she prayed deeply from her heart, she was able to find the heart of God. Her will had become God's will for her, and that's when her prayers were answered.[3]

God wants us to pray like Hannah, so deeply that we sync our wills with God's will for us. The prayer Jesus taught his disciples is to be prayed out of a deep desire for God's will to be done in the world with the understanding that we are the ones to help make it happen. To do that, we must struggle to put aside our own desires and distractions and focus on what God wants for the world that God has so lovingly created and continues to maintain. Seeking to do what God wants for creation is what will bring God's kingdom on earth as it is in heaven. That's what will revolutionize the world.

The amazing power of this prayer is unleashed through a united body of believers who do not mindlessly or selfishly repeat this prayer, but who instead pray to God with sincere desire like Hannah, with a promise to live the prayer like we really want what we're praying for to happen. We are these disciples when we learn to put God's priorities first in our lives, showing that we love God with all of our beings. When we engage in efforts to help and heal others, we show that we love them as ourselves. Only when we learn to put these top commandments first in our Christian walks—above all else—and only when we work to implement them with all of our hearts, souls, minds, and strength, will we become the kingdom builders that Jesus teaches his disciples to be.

The Power of "Our"

The word "our" is not included at the beginning of the prayer in Luke's Gospel as it is in Matthew's ("Our Father . . ."). Yet the verbs throughout Luke's prayer are plural: the unnamed disciple asks Jesus to teach "us" to pray. The other disciples would have been there right with him when he made this request. Since Matthew's Gospel includes this prayer as a part of the Sermon on the Mount, it is likely that the prayer was taught not only to the twelve disciples, but to the entire crowd following Jesus.

Jesus taught all who followed him to pray this not only individually, but to also pray it together. Throughout the long history of the church, Christians have been memorizing and repeating this prayer together, both as individuals and as bodies of believers. We love to lift up our voices and sing it together as well. I'm sure that God delights when this prayer is delivered in song, faith, and unity by a group of believers. If only we would hear God's response to go out and share God's love with the world in that same heartfelt faith and unity!

According to "Global Christianity: A Report on the Size and Distribution of the World's Christian Population," a 2010 study by the Pew Research Center's Forum on Religion

& Public Life, 2.18 billion people identified themselves as Christian around the world, which is close to one out of every three people living then. This report tells us:

> The proportion of Europeans and Americans who are Christian has dropped from 95% in 1910 to 76% in 2010 in Europe as a whole, and from 96% to 86% in the Americas as a whole. . . . At the same time, Christianity has grown enormously in sub-Saharan Africa and the Asia-Pacific region, where there were relatively few Christians at the beginning of the 20th century. . . . Christianity today—unlike a century ago—is truly a global faith.[4]

Imagine if eighty-six percent of the people living in the Americas worked together to bring the good news of God's loving and healing to the people in their lands who are poor and in need. Imagine what the world would be like if almost one out of every three persons living today truly believed that bringing God's loving and healing kingdom on earth was the most important thing they could do!

Bringing God's kingdom on earth is to be a joint goal for all Christians, working together not only with people of our faith, but with like-minded people of other faiths and even with those like-minded people who claim no faith. God's goal for us will be implemented when we unite our hearts, minds, and faith together as God's children, when we pray deeply with God's will as our only focus, and when we use the strength that God has given us to make it happen.

Uniting the Vision

The problem with so many people identifying themselves as Christians is that capturing one vision of how to put faith in action can seem impossible. The biblical record lets us know that even at the very beginning of the faith, the new Christians had differences of opinions about how to be obedient to God's will.[5]

The history of how Christianity has both multiplied and divided into different kinds of sects should help us to think more deeply about what God's plan really is for those who believe. Since I don't believe that anything God does is accidental, I've come to the conclusion that all of our divisions are to help us learn something about God's plan for us—God's plan for all who claim faith in the Christian God. We must understand that the vision that God wants for the world does not require all Christians to believe or practice their faith in the same way. God's vision for the kingdom on earth is bigger than all of our faith traditions, and is not to be controlled by any one faith group.

The question persists, however: how can Christians agree on what God's vision is for the world? As I've indicated throughout this book, Jesus has given us the information we need to understand what we are to do:

- In his first sermon, Jesus said he was anointed to preach good news to the poor, proclaim freedom for the prisoners and recovery of sight for the blind, release the oppressed, and proclaim the year of jubilee (Luke 4:16-21). We are to bring God's healing love to those who need to feel it.

- When John the Baptist sent messengers to ask Jesus whether he was the Messiah, Jesus responded by describing what he had accomplished: the blind received sight, the lame walked, the lepers were cured, the deaf heard, the dead were raised, and the good news was being preached to the poor (Luke 7:18-23). We are to be the salt of the earth, changing the "flavor" of the world through our service to others.

- Jesus taught that those who will be received into the kingdom of God in heaven are those who feed the hungry, provide drink for the thirsty, invite the stranger in, clothe those who are in need, care for the sick, and visit the prisoners. Whatever we do for "the least of these" we do for

Jesus (Matthew 25:31-46). We are to be the light of the world, shining the light that will scatter the presence of persistent poverty, oppression and evil.

- Jesus put his hands on the little children, blessed them, and refused to let the disciples shoo them away. "Let the little children come to me, and do not hinder them, for the kingdom of heaven belongs to such as these" (Matthew 19:13-15). We are to protect and care for all of God's children.

- Jesus treated women with respect and gave them authority and honor in ways that were scandalous according to the teachings of his times.[6] We are not allowed to look down on, oppress, or discriminate against anyone, ever, especially based on the circumstances of their births.

- Jesus refused to allow his disciples to destroy the Samaritans whom they hated, rebuking the disciples when they suggested it (Luke 9:51-56). He used the hated Samaritans as examples of behaviors that are pleasing to God (Luke 10:25-37; Luke 17:11-19; John 4:1-42).

- Jesus told us we are to love even our enemies, to do good to those who hate us, to bless those who curse us, and to pray for those who would abuse us (Luke 6:27-28). We are to love those whom we consider to be our enemies— they are all God's children—and we are to seek to bring the good news even to them. We must understand that our love is to be stronger than their hate.

We're taught by Jesus to focus less on satisfying our own desires and more on showing love to others, period. All of the differences in the various beliefs among Christians are irrelevant to this primary work. How much of our precious time do we spend disputing with other believers over irrelevancies! We're taught that we must all "work out [our] own salvation with fear and trembling."[7] Within our various belief systems, we are to continue to do the work Jesus has called us to as a community of people who claim to be Christians. They will know we are Christians by our love, not by our theologies.

The way we are to relate to people of other faiths is to remember that our job is to share the good news of the kingdom of God, not to force everyone to believe what we believe. We are not to judge people with different faith beliefs; that is God's job. They will either receive the good news we share or not. We can still work with them for God's purposes even if they do not want to be Christians.

To be a disciple means to learn how to love others the way Christ loves us, unconditionally. That means we are to recognize that no one is perfect. What is most important is for us to work together for the kingdom in the best way we know how with all people who are willing to join us. When we do this, I believe our nearly one-third of the world's population will increase the number of those who work for the kingdom to eventually become a majority. Then the world will truly change!

Following the Primary Example

If Jesus' teachings are not clear enough for us, the example of the first church that gathered after the Holy Spirit poured out so powerfully on Pentecost gives us the purest example of how Christianity is to work. Acts 2:42-47 tells us that the fellowship of earliest believers, some three thousand of them, was devoted to the apostle's teachings, to their gatherings, to sharing meals together, and to praying:

> All who believed were together and had all things in common; they would sell their possessions and goods and distribute the proceeds to all, as any had need. Day by day, as they spent much time together in the temple, they broke bread at home and ate their food with glad and

generous hearts, praising God and having the goodwill of all the people. And day by day the Lord added to their number those who were being saved. (Acts 2:42-47)

This example of what it means to be Christian is uncomfortable to the modern church, especially in the United States and in other capitalist countries. We shy away from the idea that we are to share all that we have so that others' needs will be met, because we have become enamored with the idea that individual accomplishment should be tied to individual wealth. To offer a vision that challenges the god of individual wealth is to speak treason in capitalist countries, so we water down our Christianity accordingly, limiting our work to providing alms and pittances for the poor. At the same time, we ignore systems that nourish and increase poverty while creating great wealth for a few. We visit the prisoners with hymns, preaching, and prayer, but do nothing to correct the unjust systems that nurture both the creation of prisoners and the business of imprisoning people. We feel no inconsistency with our faith when we rail against paying more taxes to support the poor in our communities.

I'm not proposing that the Christian church should become an advocate for any particular kind of social or economic system, including capitalism. God's vision is bigger than these human constructs. In the Americas, if all eighty-six percent of the people who claim to be Christians fully understand that God's vision for the world doesn't have any of God's people suffering from entrenched poverty, war, or disease, and if they devote themselves to living like they want that vision to become true, then they will work out a way to make the necessary societal changes no matter what social or economic system controls their countries. Don't you think if this happened, this kind of Christianity would spread like wildfire?

Jesus calls us to a radical love for God that is matched by a radical love for others. When we dilute his teachings so that we can fit comfortably in our broken societies while we claim to be his followers, we become ineffective. We become like salt that has lost its taste. There is power in the name of Jesus to break every chain! When we open our hearts and minds to the primary task of kingdom-building, the first love of Christian discipleship, we become empowered by the Holy Spirit to make great strides to make the world a better place.

Maturing in Faith

Jesus taught the disciples to pray, and then, in the teachings after the prayer, he promised them that the power of the Holy Spirit would be God's response to their heartfelt prayers. I don't believe the disciples fully understood what Jesus meant when he first taught them how to pray and what to expect from that prayer. They did not "get it" until after he rose from the grave, ascended to heaven, and poured out the Holy Spirit on them at Pentecost. When they received the power of the Holy Spirit, they were guided to act and speak with amazing power!

Don't we wish we could experience an outpouring of the Spirit like that again? I believe we can. We have been promised the presence of the Holy Spirit, and the Shekinah of God is just as powerful now as she[8] was when she poured out on Pentecost. We must understand that God did not give the disciples that power until they were fully ready to receive it. They had trained under the Master Teacher, were eyewitnesses to his death and resurrection, heard the final teachings from the arisen Christ, and witnessed his ascension before the full power of the Holy Spirit was made available to them. Like the disciples, we must grow to maturity in our faith before we can wield the kind of power God offers to us.

All believers have an individual responsibility to seek the wisdom and power that God offers to us through heartfelt prayer, devoted study, deep meditation, and selfless offering of our lives. This discipleship work is not to be secondary to our families or friends, whom we are to bring along with us if they are willing. This level of maturity is what the churches must teach all believers in order for the revolutionary power of the Lord's Prayer to change the world.

The change we work for will only happen if we truly believe this simple statement: "Jesus was right." Jesus was right in everything that he taught. He was right about how we are to relate to money. He was right about how we are to treat others. He was right about the importance of forgiving. He was right about loving God and loving others as our top priorities. We must fully understand that if we all try our best to do what Jesus taught and to follow his example, the world will become a better place; it will become God's kingdom on earth.

The revolution begins in the minds and hearts of believers who understand that we each have to do our part. We don't have to believe that anything we do will actually change the world. We have to believe that it's our job to do our part according to Jesus' teachings. How will it all come together? Well, that's what God sees, understands, and orchestrates.

Disciples who tenaciously focus on sharing God's love with the world receive several added benefits. We experience the ultimate joy of the Lord in the work that we do; we know the amazing peace that goes beyond the understanding of this world; we are driven by a purpose for living that makes life abundant—not measured by material wealth, but by love, joy, hope, and peace; and we have the comforting knowledge that we have helped to move the world to a better place—a place where one day every tongue will confess that Jesus Christ is Lord, to the glory of God the Father.

This is the true joy in life that Christ offers to dedicated disciples. And if we share this kind of joy while we're still in the world, imagine Jesus rejoicing with us when we return to him! Can you hear Jesus saying, "Well done, my good and faithful servant?" Isn't that what all of Christ's disciples should desire more than anything else in life?

Deepen

Black Lives Matter (BLM) was founded by three black community organizers in the summer of 2013.⁹ It is an international activist movement that campaigns against violence toward black people. BLM began after the acquittal of George Zimmerman for the shooting death of Trayvon Martin, an unarmed seventeen-year-old black youth visiting the housing complex that Zimmerman patrolled as a voluntary participant in a neighborhood watch program administered by local police. The movement organizes protests around the deaths of black people by police actions or while in police custody, such as Jonathan Farrel (Charlotte, NC) in 2013; Michael Brown (Ferguson, MO), Eric Garner (New York City), and Tamir Rice (Cleveland, OH) in 2014; Eric Courtney Harris (Tulsa, OK), Walter Scott (North Charleston, SC), Sandra Bland (Waller County, TX), and Freddie Gray (Baltimore, MD) in 2015; and Alton Sterling (Baton Rouge, LA), Philando Castile (Falcon Heights, MN), and Sylville Smith (Milwaukee, WI) in 2016. In the summer of 2015, Black Lives Matter began to publicly challenge politicians—including candidates in the 2016 United States presidential election—to state their positions on BLM issues.

INDIVIDUAL DEEPENING EXERCISES

1. Think about whether you truly believe that Jesus was right about all that he taught. Where do you hesitate? Why?

2. What are some needs in your local community that other groups don't seem to be addressing adequately and that your church or group may want to become involved in? What obstacles will you have to overcome to make it happen? How can you get others to help you make it happen? What is stopping you from getting started?

3. Pray for the families of the African Americans mentioned above who were fatally shot by police in the last few years; pray for the families of all the police officers who were shot in retaliation; pray for racial reconciliation in our country; pray for justice and peace to be felt by all in our country. After praying, think deeply, and pray even more deeply, about how you can help to bring social justice and healing to racial animosity, gun proliferation, and violence in our nation.

4. Pray and meditate on the author's expanded version of the Lord's Prayer, below. (You will pray it together at the end of the group session.)

May God bless you in your discipleship walks with unlimited hope, abiding peace, abundant love, and untamed joy!

The Lord's Prayer: The Disciples' Expanded Version

Abba, it is amazing that we can call you our Father, knowing that your love for us is broader and deeper than we can ever imagine and that you are always faithful to us. We love you as our beloved Papa, and yet we bow down before you because you are supremely holy and deserve more honor than we know how to give you. We offer our lives to you as your loving children for your will to be done through us. We worship you with all of our beings, for you are a loving, generous, and kind father to us all. You alone deserve all glory, honor, and majesty.

We are your disciples, God. More than anything in this world, we desire for your kingdom to come on earth as it is in heaven. We want to be able to do those "greater things" that Jesus promised we would be able to do through the power of the Holy Spirit. Help us to see the world and the people in it through your loving eyes. Please, Lord, help us to envision the kingdom you call to be created on earth.

"**Give us each day our daily bread.**" God, if you will help us by providing for our daily needs, we promise to turn our minds and hearts first and foremost to accomplishing your will. We will turn your love for us into our love for others, that others may come to know your will and be blessed. Help us to know how to live simply and how to faithfully do your will. We are here to serve you, God, so please provide us with sufficient food and shelter so that we can faithfully focus on the work you have for us. Into your hands we place our lives.

"**Forgive us our sins, for we also forgive everyone who sins against us.**" Dear God, we seek to be the loving and forgiving people you need us to be in this world. Help us to see the places where forgiveness is missing and to offer it. Help us to see the needs of others rather than their faults, their potential goodness rather than their failures, and the hope you had for them when you created them. Help us to learn how to truly forgive others as Jesus has forgiven us. Please forgive us when we are too short-sighted to understand your vision of how to love the world, when we find ourselves living in fear rather than in faith, and when we fail to be the shining lights that you expect us to be.

"**And lead us not into temptation.**" Loving Father, help us keep the view of the kingdom clearly in front of all the temptations we face. Help us to stay on the path that you have designed for us, to know the work that you call us to do, and to not fall short from doing it. Do not let the ways of the world pull us from the path, Abba God. Please strengthen our will to get up, go, and do.

"**For the kingdom and the power are yours forever.**" The kingdom that we seek is yours; the power that we wield is yours. We do everything for your glory and your honor, Lord, for you alone are worthy. In the name of our Lord and Savior, our comforter and healer, the Prince of Peace and the King of kings, Jesus the Christ, we pray. Amen.

GROUP DISCUSSION

1. Review the chapter.

(a) Discuss what it means to "sync our wills with God's will for us."

(b) Share your imaginings about what the world would be like if "almost one out of every three persons living today truly believed that bringing God's loving and healing kingdom to earth was the most important thing they could do." Discuss what kinds of things would happen in your local community and in the nation. What kinds of things would happen to Christian churches and denominations? What would non-believers begin to understand about Christianity?

(c) Discuss these statements: "We must understand that the vision that God wants for the world does not require all Christians to believe or practice their faith in the same way. God's vision for the kingdom on earth is bigger than all of our faith traditions, and is not to be controlled by any one faith group." Do you think Christians can work together if they hold different views about how to practice their faith? Do you think Christians should work with non-Christians?

(d) Do you agree or disagree with the author's suggestion that capitalist countries too often worship a "god of individual wealth"? This may be controversial to some Americans because of our history of fear and loathing for anything that may sound like communism. Remember, however, we're talking about Christian communities, not the forms of communism that were practiced in other countries during the Cold War. What makes the difference?

(e) Discuss "true joy" as proposed by the author and what it means. Have you ever done any mission or ministry work that gave you that kind of joy?

2. Share your thoughts from Individual Deepening Exercise #2. How are the needs you see in your community similar? How are they different? Discuss how you might work together to accomplish some or all of the community needs you identified.

3. Some Christians firmly believe that the church is not to be involved in politics or even to discuss political issues. Wikipedia offers a broad definition of the word *politics*: "Politics . . . is the process of making decisions applying to all members of each group."[10] A similarly broad definition found in *Webster's Unabridged Dictionary* is "the art of adjusting and ordering relationships between individuals and groups in a political community." With these definitions in mind, discuss whether churches should engage in petitioning the government on behalf of the poor and needy. Do you think such work is "too political" for churches? Do you see the claim that the church should not be involved in speaking out on social issues as a possible "veiled temptation"? Why or why not?

4. Discuss whether the church should be involved with, support, or help social movements like Black Lives Matter in any way. Would this social issue be considered "too political"? Why or why not? Where do you draw the line between social action that is appropriate for the church and social action that is "too political"?

5. As you close out this study, stand (in a circle if possible), hold hands, and read together the author's expanded Lord's Prayer on pages 123 and 124, taking your time to truly hear the words that you are praying. If it is within your tradition, share hugs before you go!

NOTES

1. Read more: https://www.washingtonpost.com/national/in-dallas
-obama-seeks-to-soothe-tensions-between-civilians-and-police
/2016/07/12/74bc5046-4871-11e6-bdb9-701687974517_story.html
?utm_term=.c43e2ed27505.

2. Ibid.

3. See 1 Samuel 1 and 2.

4. Read more: http://www.pewforum.org/2011/12/19/global
-christianity-exec/.

5. See, for example, Acts 15 where the elders of the church were divided in opinion and gathered to debate whether Gentiles must undergo circumcision to come into the Christian faith. This was a major division because of the importance of circumcision to them. Circumcision was a commandment from God to Moses, part of an "everlasting covenant" between God and God's people (see Genesis 17:9-14).

6. See, for example, Luke 10:38-42. Jesus allowed Mary to sit at his feet to learn, rather than wait on the men as women traditionally did. In those times, women were not allowed to learn as the men did, and sitting at the feet of a teacher was the posture of a rabbinic student. See also John 4:4-32, where Jesus met a Samaritan woman of questionable character at a well and asked her for a drink—a scandalous thing to do, since as a rabbi he was not allowed to talk to women or drink from a Samaritan cup. He treated her as a disciple, sending her to tell the Samaritan people about him.

7. Philippians 2:12-13: "Therefore, my beloved, just as you have always obeyed me, not only in my presence, but much more now in my absence, work out your own salvation with fear and trembling; for it is God who is at work in you, enabling you both to will and to work for his good pleasure."

8. See the discussion of the femininity of the Holy Spirit in Chapter 3, p.47.

9. Read more: http://blacklivesmatter.com.

10. Read more: https://en.wikipedia.org/wiki/Politics.

Bibliography

Boring, M. Eugene. "The Gospel of Matthew." In vol. VIII of *The New Interpreter's Bible,* edited by Leander E. Keck, Bruce C. Birch, John J. Collins, Katheryn Pfisterer Darr, Jack A. Keller Jr., William L. Lane, Thomas G. Long, James Earl Massey, Gail R. O'Day, David L. Petersen, and Marion L. Soards. Nashville: Abingdon Press, 1995.

Culpepper, R. Alan. "The Gospel of Luke." In vol. IX of *The New Interpreter's Bible,* edited by Leander E. Keck, Bruce C. Birch, John J. Collins, Katheryn Pfisterer Darr, Jack A. Keller Jr., William L. Lane, Thomas G. Long, James Earl Massey, Gail R. O'Day, David L. Petersen, and Marion L. Soards. Nashville: Abingdon Press, 1995.

Hoffmann, Oswald C. J. *The Lord's Prayer.* San Francisco: Harper & Row, 1982.

Kendall, R.T. *The Lord's Prayer: Insight and Inspiration to Draw You Closer to Him.* Grand Rapids: Baker Publishing Group, 2010.

King, Martin Luther, Jr. *Strength to Love.* New York: Harper & Row, 1963.

Mathias, Philip. *The Perfect Prayer: Search for the Kingdom through the Lord's Prayer.* Minneapolis: Augsburg Books, 2005.

Mulholland, James. *Praying Like Jesus: The Lord's Prayer in a Culture of Prosperity.* San Francisco: HarperCollins, 2001.

NIV Archaeological Study Bible. Grand Rapids: Zondervan, 2005.

Simon, Art. *Rediscovering the Lord's Prayer.* Minneapolis: Augsburg Books, 2005.

Tuck, William Powell. *The Lord's Prayer Today.* Macon, Georgia: Smith & Helwys, 2002.

Willimon, William H. and Hauerwas, Stanley. *Lord, Teach Us: The Lord's Prayer & The Christian Life.* Nashville: Abingdon Press, 1996.

Wright, N. T. *The Lord and His Prayer.* Grand Rapids: William B. Eerdmans Publishing Company, 1996.

Afterword

Someone once said that "the faith that works is the faith that works." That statement had less to do with resolving the contrast between "faith" and "works" made famous in the Letter of James in the New Testament. It rather had the force of reminding people of faith that the gift of faith, as a Divine charism, has its own spiritual, moral, and practical dynamic that cannot be stifled by any negligence or cynicism on our part. Faith puts the believer to work in ways that often exceed whatever imaginations or inclinations one may seek to engender. It comes about chiefly through the efficacy of prayer. Through the power of prayer God keeps in touch with the believer, since God always takes the initiative in any desire we have to "get in touch with God." God always acts first!

The gospel (Jesus Story) speaks to us most eloquently about the centrality of prayer in the personal life and public ministry of Jesus Christ. It created such a contagious and mystical movement of the Spirit that the disciples were moved to ask for guidance from their Master in learning how to pray. This emerged in Luke's Gospel, at least, as the "Prayer of Discipleship," commonly known as the Lord's Prayer. In it is summed up the essential ingredients of what it means to be in a filial relationship with God. It includes the unconditional demands of Christian spiritual, ethical, and moral imperatives, as well as the radical implications of the prayer itself in making a convulsive and transformative difference in the personal lives and public witness of Christians everywhere.

This is what Alice Burnette Greene strives to express, explore, and extend in her very important volume *The Revolu-*

tionary Power of the Lord's Prayer. She tells of the very simple response that Jesus gives to his disciples by outlining for them the most important affirmations and petitions addressed to God, on whom they are totally dependent. She speaks of the prayer as "short and straightforward . . . packed with amazing depth and power." It is only through a genuine and faithful commitment to that depth and power, the author suggests, that "we, as his disciples, will become the revolutionary force that Jesus always intended for us to be in this world."

Perhaps it might appear unusual for us to think of the Lord's Prayer as having "revolutionary power." The notion of "revolution" may send shrills through the minds of those who would rather prefer to maintain the status quo in whatever context they choose to sustain. But the gospel message has no such comfort, nor should Christian discipleship make peace with anything that militates against work of freedom, justice, forgiveness, and love. To that extent then, the Lord's Prayer is bound to challenge the status quo and to usher in modes of transformation, liberation, and reconciliation where sin, corruption, and injustice abound.

Through the use of contemporary anecdotes and moral narratives, along with exercises for personal deepening and group sharing, Alice Burnette Greene skillfully provides for us a most useful devotional spiritual tool that can truly revolutionize our ways of thinking, praying, and acting. This book should find its way into churches, seminaries, ministries, and organizations that are dedicated to the transformative power of prayer, and more particularly, the Lord's Prayer. A faithful use of these pages will inevitably result in the mystical experience of "tenacious love, impermeable peace, and unbounded joy"—three divinely inspiring graces that are desperately needed in our world today.

D. H. Kortright Davis, D.Phil.
Professor of Theology
Howard University School of Divinity